Merciful

BY
DIEGO MESA

Merciful
ISBN: 978-1-939570-60-4

Copyright © 2017 Diego Mesa

Published by Word and Spirit Publishing.
P.O. Box 701403
Tulsa, Oklahoma 74170
wordandspiritpublishing.com

DEDICATION

First, I would like to dedicate this book to the person that has been the most merciful to me—putting up with all my failures, flaws, shortcomings, and mistakes all of these years. He has been the most forgiving person I have ever met, never giving me what I deserve and always restoring me back to the status I had with Him before I fell or messed up. His name is Jesus, my Lord and Savior.

Thank you Jesus for your mercy that has been ridiculously generous and kind to me all my life, giving me more than I ever deserved.

CONTENTS

Introduction

In 2008 I was diagnosed with terminal stage 4 kidney cancer. Many years have come and gone since then and God has completely healed me! But while in the midst of the battle for my health and life and coming out of it, a strong resonating word rose up in me. Even now when I look back, it's still very much alive in me. When I think about the situation, I think of this word. When I think of all the good things God has blessed my life with (wife, kids, grandkids, home, friends, things), I can't help but think of this word. When I look around and see hurting, lonely, confused, fearful people I can't help but think of this word. I'm drawn to this word. When I think of all the things that have been entrusted to me (position, title, influence, opportunity, experiences, and privileges) I think of this word. The one and only word I would use to describe God is "mercy."

A few years ago I was privileged to visit with the late Oral Roberts in his home in Newport Beach, California. He was a great healing evangelist of the 1950s and built Oral Roberts University in Tulsa, Oklahoma. When I asked what one word he would use to describe God, he said "merciful." So, I'm in pretty good company.

Within this book you will discover so many others that would also describe their God as being merciful, from David to Jonah to Ruth to the prodigal to Job to Isaac to Paul and many others. May this book expand your perspective and view of who God really is. May it draw you closer to understanding God's heart toward you and others. May it give you a new deeper appreciation for who He is. May it cause you to live a stronger Christian life for His glory and pleasure. Thanks for reading it. Enjoy!

CHAPTER 1

Full of Mercy

To Him who alone does great wonders, for His mercy endures forever;

To Him who by wisdom made the heavens, for His mercy endures forever;

To Him who laid out the earth above the waters, for His mercy endures forever;

To Him who made great lights, for His mercy endures forever—

The sun to rule by day, for His mercy endures forever;

The moon and stars to rule by night, for His mercy endures forever.

Oh, give thanks to the God of heaven! For His mercy endures forever.

—PSALM 136:4-9, 26

God is a God that is full of mercy. God's nature, God's character, God's makeup, God's disposition, God's temperament, God's constitution, God's personality, God's bent, and God's leaning is merciful. He doesn't lean toward condemnation, judgment, wrath, cruelty, intolerance, meanness, or punishment.

Second Corinthians 1:3 tells us that God is the Father of mercies. Psalm 145:8-9 also says, "The Lord is gracious, and full of compassion; slow to anger, and great in mercy. The Lord is good to all, and His tender mercies are over all His works."

First, notice the phrase *Father of mercies.* This implies that as a Father toward His children, God relates to us from a merciful expression. Certainly, as a Father, He has infinitely more mercy than any natural father could ever have. As our Father, He produces, provides, initiates, and manufactures mercy.

Next, notice the word *great.* This implies that God is best, supreme, superior, and large in mercy.

Great indicates enough; a plentiful abundance; endless; bountiful; wide and large. God is the supreme source of endless and bountiful mercy.

Finally, notice the word *tender.* Tender means gentle, delicate, emotional, mild, kind, and affectionate. That's who God is today. He is a tender, merciful God. The word *mercy* means *loving kindness, gracious, tender in affection, forgiving, forbearance, and compassion.* But in the Hebrew it means *extraordinary in uncommon goodness.* To put it simply, mercy is not getting what you deserve.

You and I deserve hell. We deserve the wrath of God. We deserve the condemnation and punishment of God. We deserve to be separated and alienated from God, but mercy reached out to us and brought us close to Him. Mercy gives us opportunities and privileges, love, forgiveness, patience, and compassion. Mercy never stops being merciful.

Through Jesus, Mercy reached out and said, "I want a relationship with them." It's not because of your looks; not because of your education; not because of your skills, your ability, or your talent. God did not say, "I want to be merciful because they have a lot to offer Me; because they can do a lot for Me; or because of everything they have accomplished." No, in the midst of our waywardness, our miry-ness, our hopelessness, and our sinfulness; in our hopeless, helpless state, Mercy reached out to us and drew us near.

If you chose one word to describe God what would it be? There are so many descriptions of His character; so many facets of His person; and so many dimensions of His being, just like a diamond with countless angles, sides, and facets. I choose "merciful" or "mercy." Maybe you have another word that you would choose to describe God. Perhaps one day you will write a book and share with the world the one word you chose. I'm sure it will be equally as rich, gratifying and fulfilling as "Mercy" was for me throughout my journey.

A Ship Called Mercy

There is a humanitarian ship called *Mercy* that has visited 575 ports all over the world. Since her first voyage in 1978, *Mercy* has taken care of nearly two-and-a-half million people and has visited more than 70 nations. Basically, *Mercy* sails the seas to provide help to hurting mankind, sailing to wherever devastation has taken place—where there has been loss of life, property, homes, and livelihood. The ship never stays very long in one location, but continues to move on to the next hopeless country or people in need.

And that's the way mercy is. Mercy continues to travel. Like the traveling hospital ship that continually sails the waters, so God's mercy travels and covers all lands and all people—never stopping and never ceasing to bring mercy to those in need. And that's the way we need to be.

There's a story about the Emperor Napoleon. The mother of a soldier in Napoleon's army asked for her son to be pardoned. It was his second offense. And because it was his second offense of the same crime, he was deserving of death. Napoleon said, "Justice demands death."

She told him, "I don't want justice. I'm calling for mercy."

Napoleon answered, "He doesn't deserve mercy."

She said to him, "It wouldn't be mercy if he deserved it."

At that point, Napoleon decided to be merciful and freed the man.

And that's the way Mercy was and is to you and me. We didn't deserve to be pardoned from our sins. We were deserving of death, but mercy intervened and freed us from justice and judgment—all because of an appeal.

Forgiven, Pardoned, and Released

Have you ever been guilty of something, but then were inexplicably forgiven? Maybe you were speeding and a policeman pulled you over. You knew you were busted, and you knew he should have written you a ticket, but instead he extended mercy toward you and just gave you a warning. That's a picture of God's mercy.

Have you ever been deserving of some consequence, but were pardoned? Maybe when you were a kid you should have been punished for doing something wrong, but your parents simply pardoned you. When I was a kid, there were times that I didn't do well in school and I knew that I didn't really deserve a passing grade, but my teacher gave me a passing grade out of mercy. You might be thinking, *Wow! That explains why you are not too smart!* Maybe so, but I sure learned what it was like to receive mercy!

Have you ever been convicted of the worst, but then were released? Have you ever been busted, guilty, caught red-handed—but then forgiven? One of the greatest examples of mercy in my own life happened while I was in Bible school. During the orientation we were told about the rules that applied to all of the students. And the Bible school was very, very strict and very disciplined because all of the students were studying to become preachers. The school wanted to instill a high caliber of discipline and character. Plus, they wanted the name of the Bible school to remain strong in its character. So they told us how we were to pay our bills, how we were to treat people, how we were to drive . . . and much more. And one of the rules was, "You are not to be parked in a car with someone of the opposite sex after the sun goes down." We were told that anybody who broke that rule was immediately going to be expelled. No second chances.

So at that time, my wife, Cindy, and I were engaged to be married. We hadn't seen each other for about three months, and so she came for a visit. And we did the normal stuff—we walked the mall and we went various places, but guess where we found ourselves toward sunset? You have probably guessed—we were together in the car, parked at a park and all alone. (It was a 1970 Chevelle, and after more than thirty years of marriage, I have to admit, it would be nice to have that car again.) But I'll just be very honest with you. This was my fiancé. I loved her. She loved me. We missed each other, and we were kissing—or maybe more. The older I get, the more I seem to forget.

So the next thing I know it's dark, and by now the windows of the car were pretty steamed up. And then suddenly a car came up behind us and its lights lit up the inside of the car. And the light reflected off the rearview mirror and hit me in the face. It was really messing up my groove and my game. And then all of a sudden I remembered the rule. And I told Cindy, "We've got to go." She said, "Why?" And I explained to her the rule that I'd heard in orientation and that because I had broken it, I would be kicked out of school. And I said, "I don't know who that is. I don't know if it's a professor. I don't know if it's the dean. I don't know if it's a student. But you know what? We've just got to go." And I dropped her off at the apartment where she was staying with some girls that I knew.

The next morning I personally took it upon myself to walk into the dean's office and say, "I don't know if you heard, but before you hear . . ." And I explained to him what had happened and then I said, "I know it was a violation of the rules. And I'm here to tell you that I accept my being expelled from Bible school."

Now you've got to realize, at that point I had wanted to be a preacher for several years. It was my dream to be at that Bible school. My church had sent me there, and I was planning on returning to serve my congregation as the children's and youth pastor. A lot was riding on this. But I went to the dean's office expecting to be kicked out of school. I knew I had messed up and I walked into that office in humility. I had already rehearsed it. I would call my parents. Then I would call my pastor. I knew I would have to let everyone that was close to me know that I'd been booted out of Bible school. Not the military, a sports team, or an important company—but a Bible school. Such humiliation. But that morning the dean looked at me, and he had mercy upon me. He could see and hear my remorse, shame, and embarrassment. He heard my confession as I acknowledged my error and wrongdoing. And he smiled and said, "Just don't do it again. Now get to class."

You can imagine the emotions that ran through me. I wept as I walked to class that morning because someone could have pronounced judgment on me, but didn't. I deserved to be expelled. I had violated the rules, but this man showed me mercy, and I was freed. I was pardoned. I deserved to be kicked out, but I was restored to a place of good-standing. I deserved to be excommunicated; labeled. I deserved a record in my permanent file, but instead I was forgiven. How much more has our loving God done for us? Not once—but over and over again. Just pause for a moment and think about a situation that happened in your life where you can see that God was merciful to you. Go ahead. Stop and think of something.

The Bible talks a lot about mercy. *Mercy* is mentioned more than 276 times in the Bible. Now, we know that grace is important. But did you know that in comparison, grace is only mentioned 170 times in the Bible? Believers have been well-educated on the subject of grace; there are countless books and songs, even conventions and seminars that are dedicated to teaching about grace, but mercy doesn't get that type of attention. And yet, there are more scriptures on the subject of mercy. Just the fact that mercy is mentioned 100 times more deserves our attention.

We need to understand what mercy is. Why? Because God is a merciful God who is full of grace and very gracious to us. And while He does extend grace, His nature—the very fabric of His persona—is mercy (among other definitions). He can't give you grace if He's not first merciful. Grace is unmerited favor. He can't give you favor, He can't bless you, He can't give you strength, He can't reward you . . . until He is first merciful to you.

Mercy is often ignored, taken for granted, overlooked, and discarded. In the same way we might walk pass pennies in a parking lot and don't bother to pick them up, mercy is sometimes overlooked—until you need it. When we *need* mercy, that's when we start to pay attention to it. Please understand, I am not trying to downplay grace. I am only trying to increase our awareness of mercy. "For by grace you have been saved through faith, and that not of yourselves; it is the gift of God" (Ephesians 2:8). Thank God for His grace!

Close to Your Heart

The Bible talks about tender mercies, plenteous mercy, rich mercy, great mercy, abundant mercy, a multitude of mercy, eternal mercy, boundless mercy, enduring mercy, and sure mercy. Look at all of those amazing adjectives that show us the length, depth, height, and breadth of God's mercy. It is without end; inexhaustible; incomprehensible. It is *extraordinary* and *uncommon* goodness. All of that has been granted to us. As the book of Lamentations declares,

"The faithful love of the LORD never ends! His mercies never cease. Great is His faithfulness; His mercies begin afresh each morning. I say to myself, 'The LORD is my inheritance; therefore, I will hope in Him!'" (3:22-24 NLT). His mercy endures forever!

During the Civil War, a Union soldier was arrested as a deserter, and he was sentenced to death. He wrote a letter of appeal to President Abraham Lincoln. The letter found its way to the president's desk. Immediately Abraham Lincoln showed him mercy and pardoned him, and sent the soldier a letter in response. That soldier returned to the battlefield and was faithful to perform his duties until he died in combat. When they went through his clothes and his personal items, they checked the pocket over his breast and they found that letter, hand-signed by President Abraham Lincoln, which said that he was fully pardoned. That's where we should all keep mercy—very, very close to our hearts. If not, we'll take it for granted. Keep it close to your heart—it has been signed by our King's blood, through the power of His crucifixion!

There are six things we need to know about mercy. The first one is this: *mercy woke you up this morning*. God said His mercies are new every morning (Lamentations 3:22-24). Yes—*mercy* woke you up this morning. It wasn't the sun that woke you up. It wasn't your alarm clock. It wasn't a barking dog or your snoring mate. It wasn't your rowdy children or the loud neighbors. It wasn't the smell of breakfast cooking or the noise of the TV. And it wasn't you, either. It wasn't your giftings, skills, or strengths. When you opened your eyes today, that was an extension of God's mercy that you didn't deserve. It was Jesus' mercy that woke you up today and said, "Good morning! You get another day . . . you get another start . . . another try and more opportunities . . . a new beginning. Enjoy it!" It's a new day full of new mercies—never opened or used, brand spanking shiny and new just waiting for you to wake up, sleepyhead! So tomorrow, when you wake up, look up to heaven and say "good morning" back to God.

Second, *mercy is granted.* 1 Timothy 1:2 tells us, "May grace, mercy, and peace be granted to you from God the Father and Christ Jesus our Lord" (Weymouth). Mercy is permitted and mercy is granted and given to you today. When you took your first breath—inhaled and exhaled—that was an extension of God's mercy. When you opened your eyes and you felt something, or tasted something, or smelled something, or heard something— that was an extension of His mercy. When you had the coordination to get out of bed and put one foot in front of the other—that was an expression of God's mercy. When you fed yourself, bathed yourself, and clothed yourself—that was God's mercy. When you lifted yourself up, stood, walked, talked, drove, ran, or jumped—that was God's mercy. It wasn't you, or because of your skills or your talent. It wasn't your strength. It was God's mercy granted to you—given to you, undeserved and unearned.

Number three, *mercy kept you*. Mercy preserved you, protected you, and kept you from losing your mind in spite of all the things you have done or that have happened to you. Perhaps you drove drunk and still made it home without hurting anyone. Or maybe you took drugs, but you didn't overdose. Maybe you had sex outside of marriage, yet you avoided an unwanted pregnancy or sexually transmitted disease. Whenever you've done dangerous things or acted irresponsibly, but have not had to endure serious, life-altering consequences—that was the mercy of God. When you were reckless, dangerous, even dumb and stupid—mercy was there.

Psalm 23:6 says this, "Surely goodness and mercy shall follow me all the days of my life; and I will dwell in the house of the Lord forever." There are two angels who have been following you—the first is Mercy and the second is Goodness. These two mighty angels have been walking along with you all the days of your life, preventing and stopping terrible things from happening to you.

You are probably thinking, *But bad things* have *happened to me.*

That may be true, but maybe angels intervened when it could have been worse. Perhaps you have suffered loss, pain, suffering, and devastating heartache—but in spite of that, you are still alive and not dead. Could it be that mercy stepped in and said, "No! Stop! Halt! That's enough! That's far enough!" If we are honest with ourselves, we know that in many bad situations in our lives, things could have been a whole lot worse!

The Old Testament tells us that there was a piece of furniture in the tabernacle called the Ark of the Covenant. God chose to make the Ark of the Covenant the focal point of the tabernacle. Do you remember the movie *Raiders of the Lost Ark*? That's what it was—like a mobile church building in a structured box. But what is interesting is that the top, or lid, of the Ark of the Covenant was called the "mercy seat" and on each side of the mercy seat were two angels—which I am calling Goodness and

Mercy—watching over everything. Remember, the Ark held the Ten Commandments, or "the Law." The Law reminds us of our failures, unworthiness, inabilities, and sin. But mercy triumphs over the Law. Mercy covers the law of sin. God wanted His people to focus on mercy!

The Bible says that God gives His angels charge over you. "For he will command his angels concerning you to guard you in all your ways; they will lift you up in their hands, so that you will not strike your foot against a stone," (Psalm 91:11-12 NIV). They are ministering spirits sent forth to those that are heirs of salvation. You are alive and well today because of the mercy of God and because angels have been watching over you.

Recently, my friend, Bayless Conley, along with two other friends, were in a horrific boat accident. They were heading toward Catalina Island in California at around 20 knots when they hit a reef. Miraculously, *it just so happened* that when they hit the reef the boat did not sink and they did not fall into the ocean and drown. *It just so happened* that on Catalina Island that weekend, search and rescue teams were doing practice maneuvers. *It just so happened* that one member of Bayless' group regained consciousness and remembered the coordinates of where they were in the middle of the ocean.

Search and rescue came and delivered them to UCLA, one of the finest crises medical centers in Los Angeles. And *it just so happened* to be a hospital run by one of Bayless' members, who saw that he got the very best care. An extra fifteen minutes' delay and my friend would have bled to death.

It just so happened? No, that is mercy—the mercy of God that intervenes, intercepts, and intercedes on our behalf. Sometimes we are tempted to try and take credit for how we get out of situations or trouble. We're just so smart or so skilled; so clever or talented. But it is always only by the mercy of God. Not coincidence, luck, good fortune, or karma. There can be no doubt about it—it was God's mercy that stepped in and stopped the enemy's plan of death and destruction from coming to pass.

When I think about how many times I was stone-cold drunk and drove my '65 Volkswagen, I wonder—how did I ever make it home? How did I not kill someone? I used to do stupid things and be a daredevil when it came to drugs, and yet nothing bad ever happened to me. My wife also has an amazing testimony of how God kept her and preserved her when she was just sixteen years old and slept in parks at night and went home with strangers. All of those things are because of the mercy of God that was at work in our lives and watching over us—even before we knew Him, acknowledged Him, or called upon Him.

The fourth truth about mercy can be found in Hebrews 4:16, which says, "Let us therefore come boldly to the throne of grace, that we may obtain mercy and find grace to help in time of need."

Mercy allows you to approach God and His throne. It is what allows you to go to Jesus when you sin; when you have been disobedient and rebellious; when you have failed and messed up; when you have fallen, erred, and done something wrong. Mercy has always been ready and available to you. It is what allows you to come close to God. God says that we can come *boldly* to the throne of grace. You don't have to stand afar off from Christ. You don't have to be aloof. You don't have to be fearful. You don't have to hide. God does not distance Himself from you because you are sinful, messed up, or have failed.

Right now, you might be crying out in pain and hurt, misery and suffering; through heartache, disaster, devastation, sickness, or depression, yet mercy will always bring you to the throne of grace. Maybe you don't realize what is happening, but you can cry out to God. You can say a simple prayer, and you will be welcomed into the throne room of God and He will hear your petition.

In 1978, I was swimming in Huntingdon Beach, California, when I was hit by a riptide. I was quickly submerged and could not come up to the surface. I should have drowned. I was tumbling and tumbling and tumbling. I took that last breath and then I couldn't hold it anymore.

Though I grew up with religion and went to a religious school for eight years, I really didn't know about Jesus at that time and I wasn't saved. I had a relationship with religion, not a relationship with Jesus Christ. But I said to myself, *If there's a God, I need Him now.* Suddenly, I shot up through the water like a torpedo. The coast guard finally located me and they pulled me in. That was the mercy of God.

I was a first-class sinner (and I still am, though I am forgiven because I received Jesus Christ as my Savior and Lord) who lived an immoral, ungodly, and perverted lifestyle. Like the Apostle Paul, I was the chief of all sinners. But even though I didn't know God, I came boldly to the throne of grace, and

I cried out for help. I acknowledged my need and desire for Him and He heard me. And in spite of everything I had done, I was not disqualified from crying out for mercy and receiving it from a holy, righteous, and pure God. Wow! Isn't that a great thought? We are never disqualified from calling out for God's mercy! Because He is a merciful God, we can approach Him as sinful, dirty, filthy, ungodly people and be in the presence of a holy, pure, and righteous God. It is amazing!

One of the greatest revelations when I had terminal cancer was the mercy of God. So many times when you go through devastation, there are so many questions you can't answer. Why did it happen? How did it happen? And it challenges every scripture you know in the Bible. It challenges your theology. It challenges everything you believe. How could a good God allow this to happen? Why didn't God stop it? How could God permit it? If God's absolutely in control, then how did it happen?

But God began to reveal Himself to me as a merciful God. I was never going to be able to explain what happened and how it happened through this pea-brained mind of mine on this side of heaven, but what I could put my head around was that God was a merciful God. And because I got a revelation that God was a merciful God, I cried out in my misery. I cried out in my hopelessness.

That might be where you are today. You might be full of hopelessness, in a crisis, battling an adversity, or fighting depression, but even in the middle of all that—cry out for God's mercy. God hears the cries of His people, and mercy is granted to those that are in misery. When you cry out to God, mercy comes running—invading and engaging your circumstances. Mercy is available for every kind of misery!

That was the state David was in when he fell into sin with Bathsheba. But he prayed to God for mercy—and he needed it. If you read the story in 2 Samuel, Chapter 11, you'll see that David deserved death. He had become a murderer. David had Bathsheba's husband, Uriah the Hittite, killed to try and cover up his other sin of adultery. He was worthy of death. But the prophet Samuel said, "You're not going to die. You're going to have to reap some things that you've sown. You deserve to die, but God will allow you to live."

Psalm 51 is the prayer that David prayed to God at that critical time. He cried out and said, "God, I don't deny what I've done, and I am guilty. But I ask you to be merciful to me." And God was absolutely merciful to him—absolutely.

God is merciful to the prodigal son who deserted his father, wasted all of his wealth, and lived with the pigs. The prodigal's life got about as bad as things could be. I remember a story about my son, Adam. I had a rule with my boys that they could not date until they graduated from high school. That was the rule in my house because I do not believe that teenagers are emotionally stable enough to be dating, so I did not allow it.

But somewhere around his junior year, I found out that he had a girlfriend. So I was cleaning the pool in the backyard, and I called him out there. And we were just talking and I just started hinting that I knew something. Is there anything you want to talk to me about, Adam? *No.* Is there anything new in your life? *No.* You remember the rule on dating? *Yeah.*

In that moment, I felt like God reaching out to Adam in the Garden of Eden after he and Eve ate of the forbidden fruit of the tree. God called out, "Where are you, Adam?" even though He knew exactly where he was and exactly what had happened.

But my son didn't tell me anything. So I said, "Who's Josie?" And then all of a sudden he got quiet. He was busted, caught, nailed, and guilty, and he knew it. In that moment, I just kept quiet and after a few seconds he began to weep like a baby. He said, "Dad, I broke the rule. I have a girlfriend."

And he was broken. He was absolutely repentant. He was embarrassed and ashamed—which was far greater than just getting caught or being sorry. He said, "Whatever you want to do, I'll submit to it." And I told him what he needed to do. He'd have to break off the relationship. But I told him that was punishment enough. It was going to be tough enough to go and tell that girl it was over, and he was going to have to deal with the emotions that he had stirred up. But I pardoned him. I forgave him. All was taken care of then. There were going to be some standards and rules he was going to have to live by, but there could have been a much greater judgment. Instead, mercy was granted to him, and it was a blessing to him. The Lord knows I had already made up my mind what punishment he was going to receive and I was a little angry that he had violated the rule, but something changed the outcome of the story when I saw the depth of his sorrow and repentance. I can't help but think God is the same way. He turns the outcome of our consequences and limits the losses.

In Titus 3:5-6 we read, "Not by works of righteousness which we have done, but according to His mercy He saved us, through the washing of the regeneration and renewing of the Holy Spirit, whom He poured out on us abundantly through Jesus Christ our Savior." This is the fifth important truth about mercy.

Mercy allowed you and I to be saved. We were able to exchange heaven for hell. We exchanged our father, the devil, for our Father God. We exchanged judgment, damnation, punishment, and wrath for the reward of grace, love, and forgiveness. We exchanged lives as children of darkness to becoming children of God. We were eternally separated, lost, forgotten, and alienated. But mercy blotted, erased, covered, forgave; it paid for the sins, the iniquity, and the transgressions of you and I when we asked Jesus to save us!

We see God's mercy extended even toward the wicked cities called Sodom and Gomorrah. God was merciful. He did not want to rain down wrath. He heard the intercession of Abraham. He was long-suffering and forbearing, but the people rejected God's mercy and judgment came upon them. The

Bible also tells us about Jonah and that he didn't want to go preach to Nineveh. But God wanted Nineveh to hear the gospel and come to salvation, and unlike Sodom and Gomorrah, the people of Nineveh responded to the message Jonah delivered. They received the expression of His mercy. You need to know that God is not angry or upset with you. He's ready to extend mercy.

God even showed mercy to the generation that died in the flood of Noah. For 120 years, Noah preached God's message every day—pleading with them to repent. God could have allowed the people to experience the consequences of their lifestyle immediately, but instead he was longsuffering for more than 120 years—giving them every opportunity to repent. Another example of God's mercy being offered through salvation is the thief on the cross next to Jesus who received the promise of eternity in heaven in the last minutes of his life, though he had lived his whole lifetime as a sinner and had done something serious enough to deserve death on a cross. Mercy was given to him.

There's something in sports called a "mercy rule." If you've ever participated in little league with your children, you know there's a mercy rule. That means if a team is getting beaten badly, they stop the game. Essentially the referees say, "That's enough beating now. That's enough shame. That's enough humiliation. That's enough losing. That's enough hopelessness." And that's what God did for us through salvation. He invoked the mercy rule. He said, "That's enough humiliation. That's enough shame. That's enough condemnation now. No more losing and hopelessness for you." He called the mercy rule for you and me.

That brings us to the sixth truth about mercy. Micah 7:18 says, "Who is a God like You, pardoning iniquity and passing over the transgression of the remnant of His heritage? He does not retain His anger forever, because He delights in mercy." The question we need to ask is why some people are still experiencing humiliation, shame, and loss because of their sin, when Jesus has made a way out with mercy.

Mercy gives us a second chance, a second opportunity, and a second privilege. Remember, it wasn't you. It's not your works, your talent, or your cleverness. God gives you a do-over in your marriage. God gives you a do-over with your children. God gives you a do-over in your relationship with Him. He allows you to have another chance.

In golf, we call it a "mulligan." When you tee-off a ball and it goes in the water hazard or out of bounds, or you swing and miss the ball entirely, if you are playing with kind people, you can ask, "Can I have a mulligan?" And possibly, they will give you mercy and grant you that free stroke.

If they decide they are not going to penalize you for that stupid shot and give you a mulligan, they pretend like you never did it, and let you go ahead and tee off again. The only problem is they won't give you another mulligan, I promise you! But God does. If man can make up a mercy rule in golf, how much more will our heavenly Father let us tee off over and over again?

And that's what God gave us. He gave us a second chance. He gave Jonah a second chance. He shouldn't have gone to Jonah a second time and allowed him another opportunity to obey when Jonah ran the first time, but He did. He gave Peter a second chance after he denied the Lord. He gave Samson a second chance by returning his strength to him even after succumbing to Delilah's temptations and breaking his Nazarite vow.

Everyone loves a feel-good comeback story. What about football player Michael Vick? He broke the law and was kicked off the team. He served a sentence in prison. But Michael Vick was granted a second chance and in 2010 he was named Comeback Player of the Year.

Another example is Tommy John. In 1974 his arm went out, and he had a surgery performed that is now named after him, that gives baseball players a second chance. There are so many pitchers now who have had an injury that should have ended their careers, but they have had Tommy John surgery and sometimes come back stronger than ever before.

Endure to the End

The Bible tells us in James 5:11, "Indeed we count them blessed who endure. You have heard of the perseverance of Job and seen the end."

After all the afflictions Job suffered—boils, sickness, the deaths of his children, and losing all his wealth—he kept on going and when it was over, God showed him tremendous mercy. "Now the Lord blessed the latter days of Job more than his beginning; for he had fourteen thousand sheep, six thousand camels, one thousand yoke of oxen, and one thousand female donkeys. He also had seven sons and three daughters" (Job 42:12).

After all the trouble, after all the pain, after all the suffering—here's the end of the story: "After this Job lived one hundred and forty years, and saw his children and grandchildren for four generations. So Job died, old and full of days" (Job 42:16).

God has the same ending written for you. After all the suffering; after all the pain; after all the hopelessness; after all the misery; after all the disappointment you've been through, after all the rejections and hardships, God has an end for you, and it's intentional by the Lord. And that end is good, for God is going to be very compassionate and very merciful to you.

No matter what you are going through right now, hold this revelation close to your heart. Hold on to the truth that God's mercy brings something, gives something, releases something, and affects and changes something. It may not lessen the sting of the pain you are experiencing, but it does soothe it. It will preserve you. Mercy is the end of the story and the conclusion to your misery.

✝ Questions for Reflection

Can you think of three things God has pardoned you from without suffering penalty?

_____

_____

_____

What definition of mercy do you identify with the most?

_____

_____

_____

Can you think of a time where mercy kept you?

_____

_____

_____

What does the phrase "it just so happened" mean to you?

_____

_____

_____

How often do you approach God and what does that look like to you?

_____

_____

_____

Can you think of a time when mercy gave you a second chance?

_____

_____

_____

🙏 Questions for Life Changes

Where can I change?

_____

_____

_____

_____

What can I change?

_____

_____

_____

_____

When can I change?

_____

_____

_____

_____

How will I change?

_____

_____

_____

_____

Who will I change?

_____

_____

_____

_____

Questions for Group Study

What does "His mercies are new every morning" mean?

_____

_____

_____

What does mercy being granted to you mean?

_____

_____

_____

What does "mercy kept you" mean?

_____

_____

_____

What does "mercy allows us to approach God" mean?

_____

_____

_____

What does "chief sinner" mean?

_____

_____

_____

How do you relate to the story of Adam breaking the dating rules?

_____

_____

_____

CHAPTER 2

Rich in Mercy

But God, who is rich in mercy, because of His great love with which He loved us, even when we were dead in trespasses, made us alive together with Christ (by grace you have been saved), and raised us up together, and made us sit together in the heavenly places in Christ Jesus, that in the ages to come He might show the exceeding riches of His grace in His kindness toward us in Christ Jesus.

—EPHESIANS 2:4-7

T he phrase in verse four of this scripture, "rich in mercy," is significant. God isn't just a little rich. He's a whole lot rich. He isn't just a millionaire, or a billionaire, or a trillionaire. God's wealth is infinite—so great that it cannot be measured!

God could have used any number of terms to describe His richness. He could have said, "I'm rich in land. I'm rich in gold. I'm rich in jewels. I'm rich in possessions. I'm rich in wisdom. I'm rich in strength." But He chose to magnify one word to describe His wealth, which means He has plenty and you can't exhaust it. God wants us to focus on the fact that He is rich in *mercy*.

Many people are attracted to God because He's rich with prosperity. He's rich with good fortune. He's rich with open doors of blessings. He's rich with favor and opportunities and all of those kinds of things. And they are attractive and appealing to us. But we need to ask ourselves if we find this thing called *mercy* appealing and attractive. Does it tickle your fancy? Does it light your bic? Wow, that's an oldie! Does it wet your whistle? Does it float your boat? OK—I think you get the point. (Ha, ha, ha!)

Mercy is probably not on most people's list of top ten things they want or can't live without. For many, that list would include money, health, happiness, fame, sex, being married, kids, vacations, a successful career, food, drink, and other things we often think of as the necessities of life or greater pleasures.

But what I want you to understand is that without God's mercy I wouldn't be what I am. I wouldn't have what I have. I couldn't do what I can do. I couldn't go where I can go. I couldn't see what I see or feel what I feel. Without God's mercy, I wouldn't drive what I drive, live where I live, work where I work, know the people I know, love the people I love, or have the ability to talk, think, and walk. Without God's mercy I would be eternally separated, lost, forgotten, alienated, punished, judged, and damned. Without God's mercy, I would be dead, helpless, hopeless, and defeated.

Instead, God's mercy has given me forgiveness, justification, righteousness, glory, grace, sanctification, acceptance, adoption, salvation, compassion, kindness, goodness, and the promise of heaven—all in exchange for what I deserved: condemnation, shame, guilt, remorse, sin, disapproval, wrath, accusation, doom, and hell. Mercy cancelled the punishment that I was going to experience. Mercy silenced the guilt. Mercy paid the debt of sin. Mercy relieved the misery we all face at times—whether natural, emotional, or spiritual. Mercy delivered me from judgment. I thank God for His mercy every day. I don't know about you, but I don't want to take God's mercy for granted, nor do I want a limited supply. I want to expect more. I want more and I need more!

Usually we find rich people fascinating and attractive. We want to know about them, maybe even meet them, and hang around with them. But there is no one as rich as God. Man only has monetary wealth, but God not only has monetary wealth, He also has mercy without measure for you. His mercy is unlimited. Today, find your answer in the rich mercy of God. You can't get it anywhere else but from Him. You can't find it on the internet, google, or Walmart. He is the only source, supplier, and provider.

A Tale of Two Brothers

There were two Korean brothers who hadn't seen each other in a long time. One brother was a very successful lawyer who went on to become a judge. The other brother progressively went down the wrong road and became a criminal, eventually committing murder. That brother was caught and sent to jail, and it wasn't long before he stood before his brother, the judge.

The story caught the attention of the national news media and there were headlines everywhere about the judge and his brother, the criminal. Most thought that the judge would show kindness or favoritism toward his brother. But this was a murder trial and a matter of life or death. So after the criminal stood there and pleaded his case, his brother pronounced judgment and said, "You will be beheaded for the crime that you have committed." The criminal was sorrowful and pleaded with the judge, crying out for help, but there was nothing to be done.

Later that night, the criminal's jail cell opened up. As the guards led him out, he could see that up on a nearby hill was his brother, the judge. The criminal watched as the judge put the noose around his own neck and hung himself, while all the officials stood there and watched. The criminal was overwhelmed. He ran to them and said, "I'm Kim. I'm the guilty one! You have punished the wrong person!"

They looked at him and said, "We know no one named Kim."

"But I murdered someone."

They looked at him and said, "We know of no crime that you have committed."

That's what mercy did for us. You and I were criminals who deserved a sentence of death. Our older brother, Jesus, had to pronounce us guilty because He is a just God. But He chose to be the one to die for us in our stead. So when the accuser of the brethren stands before us and tries to remind us of what we used to be, we need to recognize that Jesus says, "I know of no crime that they have committed. I paid for it with my life."

That is the wealth of God's mercy. Our world, our government, and our society is in desperate need of it. Why? Because this world is defiant. This world has become detestable. People are dismissing God and are living lifestyles that are disrespectful to Him. When it comes to God's Word, God's ways, and God's will, the world is dishonoring, displeasing, and decaying. And the only solution is God's mercy.

Have you heard people boasting about their sin and their wrongdoing? Do they seem to revel in their perversion, arrogance, and self-righteousness? Sometimes people can be bold, brash, defiant, lawless, and rebellious. Sometimes they can be disobedient, stubborn, unyielding, and prideful. These are the very people who desperately need

God's mercy in their lives. They need to know the following Truth:

> *"For You, Lord, are good, and ready to forgive, and abundant in mercy"* (Psalm 86:5).

> *"For great is Your mercy toward me"* (Psalm 86:13).

> *"Remember, O Lord, your tender mercies"* (Psalm 25:6).

> *"The earth, O Lord, is full of Your mercy"* (Psalm 119:64).

> *"Incline your ear, and come to Me. Hear, and your soul shall live; and I will make an everlasting covenant with you—the sure mercies of David"* (Isaiah 55:3).

> *"The Lord is merciful and gracious, slow to anger, and plenteous in mercy"* (Psalm 103:8 KJV).

What do these scriptures tell us? That God is abundant in mercy, great in mercy, tender in mercy, full of mercy, and plenteous in mercy. For each one of us, there comes a day when we must acknowledge and recognize our wayward lifestyle—that we have a hardened heart and are far from God. If only we can understand that in spite of how we have lived or what we have done, we can appeal to a God who desires to be merciful toward us in extraordinary and uncommonly good fashion! Thank God for His mercy!

Mercy, Not Judgment

A lady was walking through Central Park in New York City when she saw a long line of people waiting to have their picture taken. She asked a few questions and discovered that there was a prize-winning photographer there that day. So she thought to herself, *I'm looking good today. I don't know when this opportunity is going to come again, so let me get my picture taken.* After a bit of a wait, she had her picture taken and the photographer put the photo in a manila envelope.

Pleased with herself for taking advantage of such a great opportunity, the woman went home and pulled the photo out of the manila envelope. But when she looked at it, she recoiled in disgust. "This is a professional photographer?" she cried. "I look terrible! He really messed me up!"

She marched right back to Central Park and demanded justice. "I want my money back! You are a terrible photographer!"

The photographer looked at the picture carefully and then he looked at her. And he said, "Ma'am, you don't want justice. You want mercy!"

We don't really want justice. When it comes to all of the times that we have missed it, failed, messed up, disobeyed God, or completely forgot about God, we don't want justice—we want mercy. Mercy makes our ugliness look beautiful. Mercy is the greatest makeover you can have because it doesn't cost you anything. Jesus paid for it and it will last for eternity.

The story of Sodom and Gomorrah, as mentioned earlier, is a perfect example of God's mercy. These twin cities were very much like our culture today, with every form of waywardness—literally anything that you can imagine—no morals, no standards, no integrity. If it feels good, do it. If it looks good, do it. What are morals? What is godliness? What is marriage? What is a man? What is a woman? What is righteousness?

And the LORD said, "Because the outcry against Sodom and Gomorrah is great, and because their sin is very grave, I will go down now and see whether they have done altogether according to the outcry against it that has come to Me; and if not, I will know."

So the LORD said, "If I find in Sodom fifty righteous within the city, then I will spare all the place for their sakes."

—GENESIS 18:20-21,26

Now these were not big cities, but they probably had a population of a few thousand people. And notice what God is saying, "I will hold back judgment and be merciful, even though the outcry is great and the sin is very great, for just fifty people." That's mercy.

So then the story goes on, as Abraham pleads with the Lord for His mercy on behalf of the people of Sodom and Gomorrah. "Then he said, 'Oh let not the Lord be angry, and I will speak but this once. Suppose ten are found there.' He answered, 'For the sake of ten I will not destroy it'" (Genesis 18:32 ESV).

Think about that for a minute—thousands of people were doing every sin you can imagine, much like today, but this merciful God was willing to hold back judgment against all of them just for the sake of ten people. My first point is this: the mercy of God is seen in His longsuffering, and His patience, and His forbearance toward all of mankind. God did not want to judge Sodom and Gomorrah any more than God wants to bring judgment today for our lascivious, perverted, wayward lifestyles, whether against our nation or any other. When we consider the fact that God was willing to spare Sodom and Gomorrah, we see a picture of His longsuffering.

The Bible says, "For God did not send His Son into the world to condemn the world, but that the world through Him might be saved" (John 3:17 NKJV). Do you remember the story of Jonah, who would not preach to the Ninevites, but instead, he ran in the opposite direction? God was longsuffering toward Jonah and He was longsuffering toward Nineveh, too. God was not seeking to condemn them, but to deliver them. He said, "I don't want to bring judgment. Somebody's got to go preach righteousness so they'll change."

Another example was Lot, who lived in Sodom and Gomorrah but didn't want to leave. God warned Lot that He was going to bring judgment, but he still wouldn't go. Finally, an angel had to grab him by the hand and pull him out. In the same way, through His mercy, God is absolutely patient, longsuffering, forbearing, and slow to anger toward us—even in areas where we are unwilling to leave, change, or stop our sinful behavior.

The Forbearance of God

I don't have a lot of patience or forbearance. In fact, there are some things that really annoy me. For example, when I have to stand in a long line at the DMV, or when I have to endure the tedious process of jury duty. Bumper-to-bumper traffic or someone driving slow in the fast lane is a sure bet to test my patience. I feel the same way when I'm at a restaurant and ready to order, but my server is nowhere in sight. Or waiting for my wife to get ready for us to go somewhere. Thank God for two cars—it has saved my marriage.

Sometimes we don't show a lot of forbearance. But God is not like us. I remember when my boys were young and they would do something wrong that would really upset me. Just like parents everywhere, rather than let my anger get the best of me, I would try to bring it under control and then turn to my boys and say sternly, "One . . . two . . . three!"

I want you to know that God doesn't count to ten or one hundred or one million with us. God counts in the zillions! He is eternally longsuffering toward us to get right, to leave that relationship that we shouldn't be part of, to turn away from the pornography on the Internet, to stop sleeping around, to turn away from whatever sin we struggle with. God is a forbearing God.

His forbearance is to hold something that shouldn't be withheld. To delay or detain something that should have happened. Even in my foolishness, my abuse, my neglect, and my irresponsibility when I've done things that I shouldn't have done, God has shown me incredible longsuffering, patience, and forbearance. Why is God so forbearing? We can find some clues in the parable of the fig tree found in the book of Luke.

> *He also spoke this parable: "A certain man had a fig tree planted in his vineyard, and he came seeking fruit on it and found none. Then he said to the keeper of his vineyard, 'Look, for three years I have come seeking fruit on this fig tree and find none. Cut it down; why does it use up the ground?' But he answered and said to him, 'Sir, let it alone this year also, until I dig around it*

*and fertilize it. And if it bears fruit, well.
But if not, after that you can cut it down.'"*

—LUKE 13:6-9

That fig tree should have already been bearing fruit.
But instead of cutting it down and throwing it into
the fire, God says, "I'm going to give it some more
time! I'm going to give you some more time to get
your act together, to repent, to change, to stop—
rather than bring instant judgment in that thing." He
doesn't bring instant judgment. He allows the tree
to live just a little bit longer, giving us a precious
thing called "time."

Why is God so forbearing? It is certainly not
because He is weak or that He approves of the sin
in our lives. It's not because He's not real, nor is it
because He's forgotten what we've done. Romans
2:4 says, "Or do you despise the riches of His goodness, forbearance, and longsuffering, not knowing
that the goodness of God leads you to repentance?"
There it is. Why does God not bring instant judgment when we do wrong? Why does He still give us
more chances? Why does it seem as though we can
get away with something without getting caught or
suffering any consequences? Because He wants us
to repent. God is not condoning what we're doing;

He is not ignoring it or not bothered by it. mercy and goodness is giving us the opportunity to repent—to stop, turn around, and change direction; to change our behavior, lifestyle, and thinking; to acknowledge the wrong we've done and feel broken and sorrowful over it.

The Bible also says, "But, beloved, do not forget this one thing, that with the Lord one day is as a thousand years, and a thousand years as one day. The Lord is not slack concerning his promise, as some count slackness, but is longsuffering toward us, not willing that any should perish but that all should come to repentance" (2 Peter 3:8-9). That's why God doesn't bring instant judgment. That's why we're still alive even though we're living in sin or we're not doing right. There are believers who aren't tithing. There are people in the church who aren't willing to forgive. There are people living with jealousy and covetousness in their hearts. Christians are living like the world, conforming to worldly lifestyles. But God does not want any to perish, so His mercy and forbearance encourage us to repent.

To continue in sin because of the mercy of God is the devil's logic and it is a dangerous trap, because there will be a day when His mercy ends.

For God to be a just God, there has to be an end to His mercy for you. But He still retains the ability to be merciful. It doesn't change His character; He's still merciful, but there comes a point when there must be judgment. Whatsoever a man sows, that shall he reap (Galatians 6:7). If you've been given a lifetime to repent of your sins and accept Christ but you didn't, then comes judgment, according to the Bible. "And as it is appointed for men to die once, but after this the judgment . . ." (Hebrews 9:27).

I am still amazed by how longsuffering God has been toward me. I got saved in 1978 when I was 17 years old. But I really wasn't fully committed to the Lord. I loved Jesus, and I accepted Him as my Lord and Savior. I went to church and I read my Bible, but like the rich, young ruler, I didn't commit all of my life to the Lord. There was still part of that "world" in me. And I think about some of the things that I did, even as a Christian, that should have brought instant judgment, but didn't. There is no explanation apart from the longsuffering and forbearance of God.

Of course, I still fall short of the glory of God sometimes. We all do. We can have this amazing time in the presence of God. We pray and feel so close to God. And then five minutes later we're looking at something we shouldn't be looking at. We're saying something we shouldn't be saying. We're thinking something we shouldn't be thinking. Thank God for His mercy that's so patient and longsuffering.

God's Affection and Compassion

The second thing I want you to recognize is the mercy of God as seen in His tender affection and His compassion—His compassion toward us. One of my favorite stories that deals with mercy is found in the book of Mark.

> *Now they came to Jericho. As He went out of Jericho with His disciples and a great multitude, blind Bartimaeus, the son of Timaeus, sat by the road begging. And when he heard that it was Jesus of Nazareth, he began to cry out and say, "Jesus, Son of David, have mercy on me!"*
>
> *Then many warned him to be quiet; but he cried out all the more, "Son of David, have mercy on me!"*
>
> *So Jesus stood still and commanded him to be called.*

Then they called the blind man, saying to him, "Be of good cheer. Rise, He is calling you."

And throwing aside his garment, he rose and came to Jesus.

So Jesus answered and said to him, "What do you want Me to do for you?"

The blind man said to Him, "Rabboni, that I may receive my sight."

Then Jesus said to him, "Go your way; your faith has made you well." And immediately he received his sight and followed Jesus on the road.

—Mark 10:46-52

What a great picture of Jesus' compassion. Mercy was Jesus. Mercy *is* Jesus. Mercy was passing by and blind Bartimaeus, in his sickness and his infirmity, didn't want mercy to pass by him without receiving it. So he did some amazing things.

Jesus paused. Jesus stood still. And Jesus halted. I want to challenge you for a moment. Did Jesus pause, stand still, and halt because of blind Bartimaeus' condition, his need, his pain and suffering alone? Or was it because of the plea for mercy, the prayer for mercy, the cry of mercy, and the call of mercy?

This is so important for us to understand. Because mercy is a part of Jesus' DNA. It's His persona. It's who He is. And if you can tap into understanding who He is, then you can take advantage of it. But if you limit yourself or you don't know who He is, you will limit the availability of mercy toward you. Are there people who have circumstances and conditions, but those needs are never met? Of course!

Let's look at this story again. Why did Jesus heal this man? Why did Jesus stop and respond to his need? Was it because of His blindness alone? I venture to say no. There were a lot of blind people around and they didn't get their healing. The Bible doesn't say, "All the blind people in that city were healed." Only this man was healed. Why?

We often think that God is moved to act simply by our condition or circumstances. I don't think that is the entire picture, because if that were true, then everyone would get their need met. But there's something extra here—not only the faith the Bible acknowledges that he had, but he also tapped into the mercy of God.

Appealing to God's Mercy

Jesus didn't stop because of the condition. He stopped because blind Bartimaeus said something that struck His heart. Bartimaeus appealed to His mercy—he placed a demand. The same way the woman with the issue of blood placed a demand on the power of God, this man placed a demand on the mercy of God! I believe that when you're in a place of misery that you can appeal to God in His mercy and He will stop, turn around, and He will heal and deliver you. But if you don't know that, you'll never take advantage of it.

Some people believe, "If God wants it, He'll just do it." To some extent that's true, but most of the time you have a part to play. Have you ever gotten a new bank card in the mail? When it arrives there is an activation sticker on it. Now, it's your card. It has your name on it. It says it's not going to expire for three years. You know that you have money in that account. But you can't use that card until you activate it. And that's the way it is with God sometimes. It's available to you, but you have to activate it! Call the number on the card by calling out to Jesus to be merciful to you and watch mercy turn toward you! Hosea 4:6 says, "My people perish for lack of knowledge." So many people don't know how merciful He is and so they don't enjoy the benefits and wealth of it.

There's something about activating His mercy. Psalm 40:11 says, "Do not withhold your tender mercies from me, O Lord; let Your lovingkindness and Your truth continually preserve me." David is asking for God's mercy.

He does the same thing in Psalm 27:7, "Hear, O Lord, when I cry with my voice! Have mercy also upon me" and in Psalm 85:7, "Show us Your mercy, Lord, and grant us Your salvation." We need to do the same thing and cry out to Him, "show us your mercy, God! God, we need mercy. God, we need You!"

The key is that the psalmist is *asking* for mercy. "Have mercy upon me, O God, according to Your lovingkindness; according to the multitude of Your tender mercies, blot out my transgressions" (Psalm 51:1). "Let Your tender mercies come to me, that I may live; for Your law is my delight" (Psalm 119:77).

In all of these scriptures, the psalmist placed a demand. He knew something—he saw God to be a merciful God. He saw the need for mercy, and he *activated* that mercy.

I shared in the last chapter about the time when our son broke our rule about not having a girlfriend.

He didn't confess, but when I confronted him, he admitted everything. He wept and cried and he said, "Dad, I'm guilty. And Dad, you can do whatever you want with me and I deserve it."

My son appealed to mercy. He activated my mercy. He knew his daddy was merciful and it lessoned the consequences. It didn't take everything away, but it lessoned the judgment. Mercy must be sought. We must place a demand upon mercy. That's where faith comes in, believing that God will be merciful to us. Why don't we seek God's mercy when He's so merciful?

There was a time when my wife, Cindy, and I were talking about getting a dog for our boys when they were young, and it just never happened. We were looking for a while, but we couldn't find a dog that seemed right. Then one day, I went on a run and I was heading back to the church, when I saw this little German shepherd. I'm sure he was a mix, but he looked like he was almost full bred—he was a cute little guy. He was running around on an abandoned business property without a tag, so I thought, *somebody must have dropped him off.*

But when I came up to him, he ran into the bushes—very deep and long bushes. I went after him and called, "Come on over here." I got on my knees and beckoned for him to come, but he wouldn't come out. So I put my hand in there and he growled at me. And then he tried to snap at me. This went on for a good five to ten minutes and I couldn't get this little dog to come to me. Finally, I gave up and said, "Oh well! You know, I had plans for you, dog. I wanted to take you home and take care of you and give you a better life. But if you want to stay out here with no food in the cold. . . ." Sadly, so many of us are just like that dog. God pleads with us and begs us to come home with Him; to come out of the bush we are stuck in. He waits on His knees for a long time, while we growl and snap at Him. God is a merciful God, but we won't ask Him for mercy. We would rather keep our distance and stay hidden in our lonely bush then be embraced by a loving Master.

"And in the thirty-ninth year of his reign, Asa became diseased in his feet, and his malady was severe; yet in his disease he did not seek the Lord, but the physicians" (2 Chronicles 16:12) Wow! That man was never going to get healed. The physicians couldn't help him, and he was sure to die from his sickness because he never turned to God. Yet the Bible tells us that he knew God. How is it possible that Asa wouldn't appeal to God's mercy when He's a merciful God? I'll tell you what it is. The Bible says this, "God gives more grace to the humble. Humble yourself in the sight of God, and He will lift you up" (1 Peter 5:5-6, paraphrased). The problem is that we aren't humble. We're full of pride, arrogance, and self-righteousness. That's why we don't seek a merciful God. It's because we're too proud. We don't want to humble ourselves. Humbling ourselves means we choose to depend on God, to recognize the need of God in our lives, to acknowledge that God is God and we aren't.

Jesus tells a parable in Luke 18, saying, "Two men went up to the temple to pray, one a Pharisee and the other a tax collector. The Pharisee stood and prayed thus within himself, 'God, I thank You that I am not like other men—extortioners, unjust, adulterers, or even as this tax collector. I fast twice a week; I give tithes of all that I possess.' And the tax collector, standing afar off, would not so much as raise his eyes to heaven, but beat his breast, saying, 'God, be merciful to me a sinner!' I tell you, this man went down to his house justified rather than the other; for everyone who exalts himself will be humbled, and he who humbles himself will be exalted" (Luke 18:10-14).

It takes humility to receive mercy. One definition of humility is *to be made low*. But it takes humility to appeal to His mercy. In this story, one man humbled himself; he would stand afar off and would not even look, and God was merciful to him and exalted him. The other man was proud and boasted about his self-righteousness, but he was not exalted.

Extraordinary and Uncommon Goodness

The mercy of God is extraordinary and uncommon goodness. We can read about this in Philippians chapter two. "Yet I considered it necessary to send to you Epaphroditus, my brother, fellow worker, and fellow soldier, but your messenger and the one who ministered to my need; since he was longing for you all, and was distressed because you had heard that he was sick. For indeed he was sick almost unto death; but God had mercy on him, and not only on him but on me also, lest I should have sorrow upon sorrow. Therefore I sent him the more eagerly, that when you see him again you may rejoice, and I may be less sorrowful. Receive him therefore in the Lord with all gladness, and hold such men in esteem; because for the work of Christ he came close to death, not regarding his life, to supply what was lacking in your service toward me" (Philippians 2:25-30).

God showed His extraordinary and uncommon goodness to Epaphroditus and He also showed it to Paul. The story tells us that he should have died, but he didn't. God was merciful to him. God showed amazing goodness and amazing kindness to him. There are things that should have happened in your life that didn't happen because of God's mercy; because God showed you extraordinary and uncommon goodness. You benefitted from a different outcome than you deserved. That's mercy!

Jesus is the only one deserving of the title "good." That's why in the Bible He's called the "good Shepherd," "good Teacher," "good Master," and "good God." Why? Because He is *good*.

I experienced God's extraordinary and uncommon goodness first-hand when my son, Adam, was just a little guy, about five years old. He was running down the sidewalk and he didn't see a truck in front of him. My little boy hit that truck, and my wife and I saw it with our own eyes. His head hit that truck— right on the old steel bumper that was just at the level where this little guys' head was. Then he hit his head on the concrete, and slid under the truck. I'm telling you, it was not a pretty sight. In the natural that kid was dead—the skull cracked wide open, blood all over the place.

I ran over and pulled him out from under that truck and I lifted him up. He was limp. He was lifeless. We laid him on the grass, and I laid my hands on that boy, and I prayed. I called out to God, and I asked life to come back into his body. After I prayed for him, he regained consciousness and looked up at me and said, "Daddy, are we still going to Disneyland?" The only problem we could see then was a little bump, a knot on his head. And he was worried that our plans to visit Disneyland the next day might change. That is God's extraordinary and uncommon goodness!

A caveat to this story was that we didn't have insurance at the time because of a job transition. I would not have been able to afford the medical bills that could have been incurred because of this accident, but God was merciful.

Another example occurred when I was learning to ride a mountain bike a couple of years ago. I was traveling fast through brush and trees that were very dense like I was a contestant at the X-Games or a BMX racer. I was probably descending the hill at a pace of about fifteen miles an hour and I did not see a branch that was at least four feet long sticking out. And that thing hit my arm like a deadly spear or sharp sword, bounced off my chest, and left a giant scar that I still have today. I don't know how that didn't puncture my lung—it should have killed me instantly. But I was spared—not because of my riding skills, obviously—but because of the extraordinary and uncommon goodness of God.

And that's the same story of Epaphroditus. He should have died, but God showed mercy to him and didn't allow him to die. And this is what we need to understand: mercy makes things turn out good that could have been really bad. Mercy allows you to walk away from something that should have taken you out. Mercy leaves you rejoicing when you should have been in deep sorrow. Mercy—Jesus—deserves a response. Mercy needs a response, and that response is praise. That response is a proclamation of what God has done. That response is saying, "God, only you could have done this for me and I want to say thank you."

What responsibility do you have when God has been merciful to you? Psalms 13:5 says, "But I have trusted in Your mercy; my heart shall rejoice in Your salvation. I will sing to the Lord, because He has dealt bountifully with me." What responsibility do you have? I'll tell you—you have the responsibility to praise Him and thank Him for His mercy.

God's mercy deserves a response. Have you ever given someone a very costly gift? Have you ever done something so generous for someone that there was no way they could ever repay you? Have you ever gone out of your way to do something nice for someone who didn't deserve it? Wouldn't you expect a response of some kind in those situations? When you consider all that Jesus has done for you, what kind of response do you think He deserves? You have the responsibility to acknowledge what He has done for you. To tell anyone who will listen, "I'm alive today because of the mercy of God." Not long ago I heard that the word "mercy" in Farsi is "thank you!" You have the responsibility to serve Him and thank Him for the rest of your life.

We need to live in constant awareness of the need for God's mercy in our lives, and not allow ourselves to become arrogant and self-righteous to think that we don't need it. We should not be crying out for more fun, pleasure, or prosperity, but for mercy. The greatest need in life is not water and food, marriage or a family, or a new car and house. The greatest need you have is to receive more of the mercy of God in your life!

✝ Questions for Reflection

In what ways has God been rich in mercy toward you?

_____

_____

_____

When did mercy step in and what did it do for you?

_____

_____

_____

Where has counting to a zillion towards you been an unmerited blessing?

_____

_____

_____

Have you ever cried out for mercy? Where and when?

_____

_____

_____

What does the story of the little abandoned lost dog mean to you?

_____

_____

_____

What does humility mean to you?

_____

_____

_____

Like the Adam story, can you think of something similar that happened or didn't happen to you?

_____

_____

_____

Questions for Life Changes

Where can I change?

_____

_____

_____

What can I change?

_____

_____

_____

When can I change?

_____

_____

_____

How can I change?

_____

_____

_____

Who can I change?

_____

_____

_____

Questions for Group Study

How rich in mercy is God?

_____

_____

_____

Why does our world and society need God's mercy?

_____

_____

_____

What is the difference between mercy and judgment?

_____

_____

_____

What do the fig tree, Sodom and Gomorrah, and Nineveh have in common?

_____

_____

_____

What do you think about mercy as it relates to the story of blind Bartimaeus?

_____

_____

_____

Does God just react to need or is there something else sometimes required? What is it?

_____

_____

_____

What is the meaning of the story of the lost dog in the bushes?

_____

_____

_____

What is humility?

_____

_____

_____

The story of Epaphroditus shows what?

_____

_____

_____

CHAPTER 3

Introduced by Mercy

How often do we use an expression of "mercy" in our everyday lives? We'll say "have mercy" or "may the Lord give you traveling mercies." There was a television program called *Full House* where a character named Uncle Jesse would always say "Have mercy!" But what does it really mean when we define mercy? In the first chapter, I mentioned how much we love the word "grace." We sing songs about grace. We write books and listen to great sermons about grace—and we should. But rarely, if ever, does "mercy" receive the same attention or recognition—even though it appears in the Bible 100 times more than "grace."

Mercy is not getting what you deserve. Mercy is God's loving-kindness, forbearance, longsuffering, and compassion that He gives to us. God introduces Himself to His people through mercy. Notice what He says in Exodus 34:5, "Now the Lord descended in the cloud and stood with him there, and proclaimed the name of the Lord."

In other words, He's going to introduce himself. An introduction tells who someone really is, what you can expect from them, and how to receive from them. If you were to introduce yourself to someone, how would you do it? Would you talk about what you look like? Your nationality? Would you talk about what you do for a living? Would you talk about who you're married to? How many kids you have? I'm sure many of those things would be part of your introduction.

But how does God introduce Himself? We read in two passages how God is introduced. Exodus 34:6 "And the Lord passed before him and proclaimed The Lord, the Lord God....", and Exodus 3:14 "And God said to Moses, 1 AM WHO I AM....". God expresses Himself in several terms throughout the bible to describe His characteristics. "The Lord God": combines two characteristics which gives us Adonai, Elohim and "I Am Who I Am", reveals His Divine name declaring His character and attributes. That God is self-existent, eternal and unchangeable. This is the most holy name of the Lord, which we translate in modern days to mean Jehovah, Grace-Giver, and God of covenant. Notice in Exodus 34:6 He uses His name twice to introduce Himself," The Lord, the Lord God, merciful, and gracious, longsuffering, and abounding in goodness and truth, keeping mercy for thousands, forgiving iniquity and transgression and sin, by no means clearing the guilty, visiting the iniquity of the fathers upon the children and the children's children to the third and fourth generation" (Exodus 34:6-7). I find it fascinating that God chooses to pronounce Himself, introduce Himself, and announce Himself with the intention of us having an expectation, expression, and impression of Him as a *merciful* God. It's how He wants to be known and remembered.

I love all the prefixes to the word *mercy* found in the Word of God. It talks about abundant mercy, great mercy, tender mercy, being full of mercy, sure mercy, plenteous in mercy, numerous, rich, enduring, and everlasting mercy. These beautiful adjectives God uses to describe His mercy are comforting—knowing that He transcends anything and everything we can ever imagine.

We read throughout the Bible, time and time again, that when God's people are desperate and destitute, they cry out to Him. They repent and God demonstrates His abundant tender mercy to His people. Could it be that to receive God's great abundant mercies we must position ourselves horizontally? There must be a heartfelt cry for mercy; a recognition that we've tried everything but nothing is any better. We must come to the end of ourselves, humble ourselves, and cry out for mercy. But I do not believe that we are praying enough for God's mercy. And I do not believe that we are praising enough for God's mercy.

Which leads me to the next point. I do not believe we Christians—saints, the Church, believers—are praying enough for God to have mercy on our nation, mercy on sinners, mercy on our families, and mercy on our lives. And I don't believe that we are praising God enough for His mercy because where there is no appreciation of something, abuse will take place. And what you do not recognize and acknowledge you will not celebrate and can neglect. Why do we not celebrate mercy? Because we don't acknowledge mercy.

Psalm 4:1 says, "Hear me when I call, O God of my righteousness! You have relieved me in my distress; Have mercy on me, and hear my prayer." Chapter six, verse 2 says, "Have mercy on me, O Lord, for I am weak; O Lord, heal me, for my bones are troubled."

These scriptures should be appealing to us from a state of misery or a state of need. They trust in God's mercy and that God is going to answer. Psalm 9:13 says, "Have mercy on me, O Lord! Consider my trouble from those who hate me." There is no time to pray for mercy like when you and I are in trouble.

Psalms 25 says, "Remember, O Lord, Your tender mercies and Your loving kindnesses, for they are from old. Do not remember the sins of my youth, nor my transgressions; according to Your mercy remember me, for Your goodness' sake, O Lord. . . . Turn Yourself to me, and have mercy on me, for I am desolate and afflicted." (Psalm 25:6-7,16). Finally, Psalms 30:10 says, "Hear, O Lord, and have mercy on me; Lord, be my helper!"

We all have received God's mercy, but I believe God has even more available to meet our needs—we just need to continue asking.

The Mercy Test

Have you ever seen one of those dog rescue shows where a dog is being abused by its master? It may have been chained up and left for so long that the dog's skin has grown around the chain. The dog is emaciated. It's dehydrated. It's covered with ticks. But then the animal rescue comes and rescues the dog. They take it to a shelter and give it vaccinations. They perform surgery to remove the chain. They comb out the matted fur and give the animal a warm bed. And they are doing all of these things with the goal of putting that dog up for adoption, because they don't want it to be killed.

But one of the ways they test to see whether that dog can ever be adopted is how it responds when it is fed. Will it attack the handler when it's being fed? Or will it welcome the attention and care? So, they put the food in front of the dog and with a long extended hand, they touch the animal or reach for the food. If the dog growls or bites at the hand, and does so continually, then they have to euthanize the dog because it's not adoptable. But if the dog responds positively and shows gratitude for the food and care and mercy it has received, then there is hope that he can trust and bond with a new owner. That is a great picture of the way mercy comes to us.

Jesus Christ found us when we were bound in sin. We were chained. Our lives were filled with all kinds of issues, whether they were spiritual ticks or disease, or whatever they might be. We had a hunger in our lives. We ate, but we were not satisfied. We had no direction. We were homeless, and God took us in and He ministered the life of Heaven to us. But if His mercy does not change the nature that we once had, then we can never appreciate what we have been given. If we are recipients of God's mercy, should we not live a merciful life? Should we not be a living picture of it? So many people have been granted mercy, but they don't change—the same way some dogs do not change. Jesus is reaching out with His blood-stained hands to introduce Himself as mercy to you. Take hold of Him and let the revelation of how merciful Jesus has been to you alter and change your heart and lifestyle forever.

Mercy Pronounces Itself

There are several characteristics of mercy that we need to be familiar with, and they all begin with the letter "P." I have already mentioned the first one, which is that mercy *pronounces* itself. Remember, God chooses to pronounce Himself, introduce

Himself, and announce Himself as a *merciful* God. He *is* mercy. And it is because mercy pronounces and introduces itself that we should be drawn into a relationship with God.

The next characteristic of mercy is found in 1 Timothy 1:13-15. Paul begins to describe his life, what he was like—much like you and I—before he came to Christ. He said, "I was formerly a blasphemer, a persecutor. I killed Christians. And I was angry. A man full of rage, an insolent man. But I obtained mercy because I did it ignorantly in unbelief. And the grace of our Lord was exceedingly abundant with faith and with love, which are in Christ Jesus. This is a faithful saying and worthy of all acceptance, that Christ Jesus came into the world to save sinners, of who I am chief" (paraphrased).

Notice here that Paul begins by saying, "Although I was formerly. . . ." Were you "formerly" something before you met Christ? Are you "presently" something if you aren't in a relationship with Jesus Christ? I know I was. We weren't always saved. All of us were formerly a sinner, a prostitute, a pimp, a lesbian, a homosexual, a drunkard, a drug addict, a liar, a cheat, full of anger, a racist, or a bigot. That's what we were formerly. And I love what Paul says, that he was chief of all sinners!

I believe that about myself—as all of us should. Do you think that Paul was the greatest sinner that ever walked the face of this earth? No, he wasn't. But he is not speaking in false humility, either. He knew that each one of us is responsible for putting Christ on the cross, through our individual sins, because we were so far from God's holiness, and because we never acknowledged our need for Jesus to be our Savior. It doesn't matter if you've never cussed, never drank, or never cheated. It doesn't matter if you have never lied, stolen, or hurt anyone. It doesn't matter if you were raised in church, have a Christian name, or were baptized as a baby. The bible is clear, "He saved us, not on the basis of deeds which we have done in righteousness, but according to His mercy by the washing of regeneration, and renewing by he Holy Spirit." Titus 3:5 It's that simple. For that reason alone we all ought to say, "I am the chief of all sinners." It keeps us humble. It keeps us repentant. It keeps us broken. It keeps us grateful.

Paul goes on to say, "However, for this reason I obtained mercy, that in me first Jesus Christ might show all longsuffering, as a pattern to those who are going to believe on Him for everlasting life" (1 Timothy 1:16). That brings us to the next characteristic of mercy. . . .

Mercy Pardons

Mercy **pardons** us from our sins—the penalty, the judgment, the wrath, the damnation. Mercy pardons us from every past fear, shame, regret, embarrassment, insecurity, and condemnation. Do you know why people sometimes abuse drugs or drink too much alcohol? Why they abuse their bodies or lay down with every man or woman they meet? Why they're walking around in a constant rage? Because they have no answer. There's no therapist or psychologist that can help them with the shame, guilt, remorse, regret, embarrassment, and condemnation of their pasts. They're dealing with insecurities and fears. But through the acceptance of Jesus—when we obtain mercy through salvation—Jesus sets us free from all of that junk. Mercy pardons it all.

Maybe you really need to hear that right now, because you think that the chain is still around you, but the chain is really gone. It's like the story of the baby elephant that was chained to a pole. He tries to break free but can't pull himself away from that pole because he's little. But as he grows, that simple chain is still around his leg and still controls him, even though that big, fully-grown elephant now weighs several tons and could easily overpower any simple restraint and break free. He has the freedom and strength to go wherever he wants to go, but that elephant will not go beyond the small perimeter because in his mind he is still bound by that chain.

There are many people like that. Mercy has pardoned you and set you free from your chains, but you're still bound in your mind by insecurity, fear, shame, and condemnation for the things that you did when you were 5, 16, 27, 45, or even last night. But if you asked Jesus for forgiveness; if you cried out and repented—then God forgave you! He has pardoned you. So here's the truth: if He forgave you, you need to forgive yourself.

You know, I went to Catholic school. And I don't think it's the same now, but back in the day they had a system to punish you if you messed up. First, they would make you write on the chalkboard hundreds of times in front of the class, "I will not . . . I will not . . . I will not . . ." Just fill in the blank with whatever infraction you had committed.

The second thing they would make you do is stand in the corner in front of the class when you were bad. "Diego, go stand in the corner!" I heard that more times than I care to remember. The class instruction would go on, but there I was standing in the corner. The third thing they would do is get a giant chair and make you sit in that chair with a dunce hat on your head in front of the whole class, and they'd laugh at you. That's what they figured was the best way to discipline someone—with humiliation. I have no bitterness. I'm only sharing this as an example that I can relate to.

But I thank God for pardoning my sins. Never again will I experience the humiliation of the life that I deserved. Maybe you've heard the story that was broadcasted by CNN concerning a man who was released from prison after serving 30 years on death row. In 1983, Glen Ford was accused of killing a woman and convicted in a court of law, but in reality he was innocent, and he was pardoned 30 years later. That's what Jesus does for us—and we aren't even innocent! It doesn't matter what crime or sin we have committed, God pardons us and sets us free from the most perverted, wicked, immoral, and bad decisions we've made, along with the life sentence we are serving.

Again, the scripture says we obtain mercy. We don't earn it, deserve it, or buy it. We obtain it like an inherited name. You didn't purchase your last name. You obtained it or inherited it through a relationship. You receive God's mercy in the same way!

Mercy Provides

The next "P" characteristic that we need to recognize is this: mercy **provides** for our needs. We find an example of this in Genesis 24. Abraham is getting old, and his son, Isaac, has a need—he needs a wife.

"Then the man bowed down his head and worshipped the Lord. And he said, 'Blessed be the Lord God of my master Abraham, who has not forsaken His mercy and His truth toward my master. As for me, being on the way, the Lord led me to the house of my master's brethren.' . . . Then Isaac brought her into his mother Sarah's tent; and he took Rebekah and she became his wife, and he loved her" (Genesis 24:26-27,67).

Abraham sent his servant out in search of a wife for Isaac, and we read it was an *act of mercy.* Finding a wife is an act of mercy. We husbands need to hear that more often. Finding or having a wife is an expression of God's mercy—not misery. The Bible tells us that Isaac was hurting. He was grieving and discouraged because his mother, Sarah, had died. But God's mercy provided what he needed. When Rebekah, his wife, arrived, he brought her into his mother's tent and he was finally comforted.

And that's what mercy does. It comforts you from all the grief, depression, and pain that's in your life—all the cares you are dealing with; your deepest hurts, pains, and needs.

I remember God meeting a need in my life. When I started in ministry in 1985, I was 24 years old and I was making $300 a week; just $1200 a month. I had a wife and one kid, and two more would follow. Fifty percent of my income went toward our apartment. We had to survive on the rest. There was no way in the natural that I was ever going to have a house with that income. We didn't have any savings at all—we were just living paycheck to paycheck.

Then one day a man came up to me and said, "The Lord put it on my heart to give you the down payment to buy a house." Can you believe that man gave me $7,000? I wept and I cried with my wife. We bought a home in Fontana, California—the home where we later started our church. It cost $110,000 and we put $7,000 down because somebody met a need in our life—a longing and an aching in our life. God is merciful and mercy provides. Whether He does it sovereignly or whether He does it through somebody else, God is merciful.

Mercy Protects

The next characteristic we need to know is that mercy **protects** us from all types of things—misjudgments, danger, accidents, mishaps, and misfortunes. In Genesis 19 we read about the destruction of Sodom and Gomorrah. But before God destroyed the cities, He sent two angels to rescue Lot and his family.

"When the morning dawned, the angels urged Lot to hurry, saying, 'Arise, take your wife and your two daughters who are here, lest you be consumed in the punishment of the city.' And while he lingered, the men took hold of his hand, his wife's hand, and the hands of his two daughters, the Lord being merciful to him, and they brought him out and set him outside the city" (Genesis 19:15-16).

Wow! What a picture of mercy! How many times has God's mercy brought you out of a situation and set you somewhere safe? That's what He did for Lot, and that's what He did for Lot's family. Mercy brought them out and protected them. God directed all that energy and all that power for just these few people. And that is how much He loves us.

We can find another example of mercy's protection in Exodus 2:2, where we read about how God hid and protected Moses while Pharaoh was killing all the Hebrew babies. God's protection can hide you so that the enemy and certain dangers can't come upon you.

When Cindy and I got married, first I flew back from Oklahoma, we had the ceremony, and then a few days later we rented a U-Haul to move all our things into the apartment that was waiting for us. The only problem was I only needed about a 12-foot U-Haul because we didn't have a lot of stuff, but they didn't have one. All they had available was the largest size, which was a 28-foot truck.

Now, if you aren't used to driving big trucks like that, then you sure aren't going to make any quick turns and you had better pay attention to those rearview mirrors—that truck is long. It feels like driving a house and I felt very small—like a child behind the steering wheel, with my hands frozen in the 10 and 2 position.

So I'm driving that thing, but I was very, very irresponsible because I should have stopped to rest. Instead, I drove 32 hours straight because I'm the macho man; because I can handle it; because I think I'm invincible; because I'm a tough guy! And so somewhere outside of Albuquerque, New Mexico, I began to fall asleep at the wheel with my beautiful new bride sitting next to me. Well, the next thing I know, I went off the road and down into a giant ravine. The truck starts to tip on its side and I was driving on two wheels in that U-Haul. Now, if not for the mercy of God there could have been a horrible tragedy that day. But something pushed that thing back over onto the road and it sure wasn't my driving skills with a 28-foot truck. When Cindy woke up from her nap, I played it off like most men do. "What happened," she asked. "Nothing, honey, go back to sleep," I answered. But inside I was shaking like a leaf.

That's what mercy does sometimes—it protects us even in our stupidity and our irresponsibility. Mercy prevents something that should have, could have, or would have happened from happening. And mercy minimizes some things that could have been devastating.

We read in 2 Samuel 24:14, "And David said to God, 'I am in great distress. Please let us fall into the hand of the Lord, for His mercies are great; but do not let me fall into the hand of man.'" At this point in David's life, God was angry with David because he had sinned. He fell prey to the old sin of pride and arrogance by ordering that a census be taken so he could prove how big his kingdom was and how important he was as king. His right hand man, Joab, tried to warn him and said, "You don't need to do this. You are already a righteous man. God has already blessed you." But David's arrogance moved him to do it and God said it was sin.

The prophet, Gad, comes and tells David of his disobedience and warns him that there are three things that could happen as punishment. A seven year famine, the enemy would pursue him for three months or three days of pestilence. And what we just read was David's answer to God. Basically, he said, "If judgment has to take place, I'd rather turn that decision over to you because I don't want to be in the hands of someone else. I know God is merciful."

David knew that God was just. But he also knew that even in the process of bringing consequences into his life, God still loved him and would be merciful. David knew that God would still have his welfare and well-being in mind. It is so important that we understand the nature of God. Even when He has to chasten us, just like any good parent, He still affirms us as His children and reassures us of His love.

Several years ago, I remember when I worked for another church, and back then they had ridiculously long meetings. Church went on for hours, and I was the assistant pastor, so I couldn't leave until everyone was gone and all the doors were locked. I was the last man. I was always the first man there and the last man to leave.

One night after church, I was driving home at one in the morning and I was almost out of gas, so I stopped at a gas station. Back then, gas stations were all locked up late at night, so you had to deal with people through a window and you always had to pay with cash.

So I pulled up to the pump, and I noticed out of the corner of my eye that there was another car beyond the next pump. But I wasn't really paying attention to that—I was tired and I just wanted to get home. I walked up to the window and looked down to pull out my money. Then I glanced up and the attendant behind the window was staring at me with fear on his face. Suddenly he motioned with his hand for me to stop. So I stopped. Then he looked to my left, and I noticed there was somebody moving back there behind the pumps, but I couldn't see who it was.

I turned and took a step toward the pump and sure enough, I saw a man standing there—only he had the same fear on his face that the attendant did.

And then all of a sudden he turned around and got in the car and squealed away.

Now listen, I may be a "big" Mexican at 5'8¾" and when I'm wearing cowboy boots I'm 5'9," but I knew that my impressive physical size didn't scare that guy away. So I went back to the window and asked, "What just happened?"

The attendant said, "The guy had a gun. He was about ready to rob me, but for some reason when he saw you, he just stopped and went away."

To this day, I still believe that was the mercy of God. I don't know what he saw. But I didn't scare him. He saw something that scared him and made him drive away. Maybe it was that angel we made mentioned of before that follows us all the days of our lives called goodness and mercy. That's the mercy of God. Mercy protects, and mercy prevents.

Mercy Will Preserve You

We find an example of the next characteristic of mercy in the story of Ruth. "Now the two of them went until they came to Bethlehem. And it happened, when they had come to Bethlehem, that all the city was excited because of them; and the women said, "Is this Naomi?" (Ruth 1:19)

"Then she left, and went and gleaned in the field after the reapers. And she happened to come to the part of the field belonging to Boaz, who was of the family of Elimelech" (Ruth 2:3). "And Ruth the Moabitess said, 'He also said to me, "You shall stay close by my young men until they have finished all my harvest""" (Ruth 2:21).

Where is mercy in this story? Mercy is here in that it preserves us and keeps us from something that should have been destroyed, lost, wiped away, disintegrated, demolished, dropped, forgotten, dismissed, broken, or fallen apart. Mercy kept Ruth and Naomi. After the devastation of losing their husbands, mercy allowed them to go back to Jerusalem to be welcomed and received by family, to find a job, to find somebody that would bless them with more than they could ever imagine, to eventually provide a husband for Ruth and then a child.

All of that is a picture of God's mercy. God could have forsaken them. God could have forgotten about them. God could have left them alone or left them out, but His mercy reached out and preserved them. Preservation is when God keeps you well. He keeps you sheltered. He keeps you safe. He keeps you shielded. He keeps you secure. He conceals you from damaging and toxic things that can harm you. He keeps you together—intact.

When you should have fallen apart when you went through that divorce; when you should have fallen apart when you lost your job; when you should have fallen apart when you lost your child; when you should have fallen apart based upon what happened to you; when you should be harboring resentment; when you should be damaged beyond repair . . . you may find yourself wondering, *How do I still have my emotions? How do I still have my mental stability? How do I still have love and grace in my heart even after what someone has done to me? How can I love my natural father after what he did to me?* So many Christians have mercy at work in their lives—the mercy of God that preserved their emotions, or preserved their mind, or preserved their health, or preserved their marriage, or preserved their faith.

The Bible says in 2 Timothy, "The Lord grant mercy to the household of Onesiphorus, for he often refreshed me, and was not ashamed of my chain; but when he arrived in Rome, he sought me out very zealously and found me. The Lord grant to him that he may find mercy from the Lord in that Day" (2 Timothy 1:16-18).

We preserve jellies and jams. We preserve fruits and pickles. God can preserve you. I am in awe when I think about how God preserved my ministry. None of it should exist based on what I have gone through in my life—being kicked out of the church; I had nothing, no provisions, and nobody to mentor me. I had no one to speak into my life, and yet God has been so merciful to me and to the church I am blessed to pastor.

Psalm 121:7-8 says, "The Lord shall preserve you from all evil; He shall preserve your soul. The Lord shall preserve your going out and your coming in from this time forth, and even forevermore." God has the ability to preserve you. Don't be over-whelmed because of where you are today. God can preserve you. He can keep you.

"King Hazael of Aram had oppressed Israel during the entire reign of King Jehoahaz. But the LORD was gracious and merciful to the people of Israel, and they were not totally destroyed" (2 Kings 13:22-23 NLT).

The words "oppressed" and "not totally destroyed" are important here. The Bible says the people of Israel were oppressed—so they were going to go through difficulty, but they were not going to be totally destroyed. If we look at mercy and all of its pardons, provisions, protections, and preservations—are these characteristics all-encompassing, all-inclusive, and always absolute? No. But God still is merciful.

Right now you may be thinking, *It's wonderful of you to tell the story about the U-Haul. It's wonderful of you to tell the story at the gas station, but let me tell you what happened to me or my family when we needed mercy and it did not come.*

It's easy to look at the circumstances in your life or the lives of those you love and find reasons to say, "God is not merciful." But He is. How many times do we hear people say, "If there's a God, why did He allow this? Why did He permit this? If God's so loving, if God's so merciful, why did this happen?"

Let's be honest—we've all had that thought at one time or another. But just because something bad happens, it does not take away from God's loving-kindness or His mercy. That's what we need to understand from this scripture in 2 Kings. Oppression took place. God could have taken away the oppression, but He didn't. But He still extends His mercy, so they were not completely destroyed.

The truth is that if we suggest that God isn't merciful because of some loss or something that happened, then we are implying that God is not just. We're implying that we know everything about that situation and we don't. As long as we're on this planet, the Bible says we see in part and know in part (see 1 Corinthians 13:9,12). Too often we try to judge a situation through dirty glasses and we can't. We try to judge some earthly thing, but we don't have a heavenly perspective. But on the other hand, heaven is judging this thing and can see it perfectly.

For example, let's consider what might happen if someone you know dies in a car accident. Your first response might be to get mad at God and want to know why God permitted that horrible thing to happen. It's easy to then start thinking that God is not loving; that He's not merciful or to question His integrity. Really? Do you know everything about the situation to judge it? You don't. You don't know what that person was thinking. You don't know what they were doing. You don't know where their faith was. You don't know what their lifestyle was like. You don't know how many times God warned them.

Here's what I want you to see. God is always just. If He ceases to be just, He will not be God. So if someone died before their time, God was just—and He was still merciful. If that loved one is in heaven, is that not an act of mercy? Because none of us deserve to go to heaven. And God allowed your loved one to go to heaven. I promise you, no one in heaven is telling God, "You weren't merciful! You should have given me another 20 years!"

No, they're saying, "Thank You, God, that Your mercy allowed me to come into this place!" They are reunited with loved ones and saying, "Hasn't God been merciful that He allowed us to be together again? Has He not been merciful to reward us for what we don't deserve and give us Heaven, and then allow us to see Jesus?" No one who is in heaven thinks God was unjust to them.

So never judge your hardship, even though it may not make sense to you and still hurt. It would be like you sitting in the outfield bleachers of a baseball stadium and trying to call the play at home plate. "They're out! I know they were out!" But then they show the instant replay on the giant screen and you see they were safe the whole time. Don't sit in the bleachers trying to judge home plate. Let the umpire who's right there make the call, "You're safe!"

God is the umpire. He's just. He knows what is good.

✝ Questions for Reflection

Is mercy part of your vocabulary? How do you use it?

_____

_____

_____

What does the dog analogy mean to you?

_____

_____

_____

Can you think of things that mercy pardoned you of?

_____

_____

_____

What has God provided through mercy to you?

_____

_____

_____

Where has God's mercy protected you?

_____

_____

_____

Where has mercy preserved you?

_____

_____

_____

🙏 Questions for Life Changes

Where can I change?

_____

_____

_____

What can I change?

_____

_____

_____

When can I change?

_____

_____

_____

How can I change

_____

_____

_____

Who can I change?

_____

_____

_____

Questions for Group Study

How many times is grace versus mercy found in the Bible? Why is this significant?

_____

_____

_____

How one introduces himself or herself is an indication of what?

_____

_____

_____

What does the dog analogy describe about mercy?

_____

_____

_____

How can you relate to Paul's statement of a former identity?

_____

_____

_____

What are the ways that God's mercy provides?

_____

_____

_____

How has God protected us?

_____

_____

_____

How has mercy preserved us?

_____

_____

_____

Why do people think God has not been merciful to them?

_____

_____

_____

CHAPTER 4

The Companions
of Mercy

The Bible tells us in Psalm 94:18, "If I say, 'My foot slips,' Your mercy, O Lord, will hold me up." The New Living Translation reads, "I cried out, 'I am slipping!' but your unfailing love, O Lord, supported me." And also, in the Amplified version, that same scripture says, "When I said, 'My foot is slipping,' Your mercy and loving-kindness, O Lord, held me up."

I wonder how many times God has done things for us that we're not even aware of because of mercy. I wonder how many times Jesus has done things for us that we didn't acknowledge or thank

Him for. I wonder how many things God has done for us but we took the credit for it instead of thanking Him.

A few years ago a movie came out called *Les Miserables*, starring Hugh Jackman and Russell Crowe, based on a book written in 1862 by Victor Hugo. If you have never seen the movie or read the book, *Les Miserables* is a great picture of mercy. The story centers around a character who was in prison. He was labeled a criminal. He was given a number. Nobody wanted anything to do with him. Because of that he became cold. He became hard. He became mean-spirited.

But then he was released from prison and the monsignor took him in and gave him a warm bed and fed him; he loved him and encouraged him. Then one night the criminal stole a bunch of silver pieces and took off. When the police caught him and hauled him back to the monsignor, the monsignor didn't press charges, but showed him mercy. In fact, he said, "You know what? Those weren't stolen. Those were gifts that I gave him." And he told the criminal, "You forgot to take the candlesticks."

That act of mercy finally reached that criminal's hardened heart—and it changed him. He took care of a prostitute. He took care of the daughter of the prostitute for the rest of his life.

It's a great picture of what Jesus did for us. He could have judged us. He could have condemned us. He could have punished us. We became cold and hard because of our sin, but mercy was extended to us. And hopefully, that mercy has changed your life like it has changed mine.

Mercy and Goodness

In Exodus 34:5-6 we read, "Now the LORD descended in the cloud and stood with him there, and proclaimed the name of the LORD. And the LORD passed before him and proclaimed, 'The LORD, the LORD God, merciful and gracious, longsuffering, and abounding in goodness and truth."

Throughout the Bible we find scriptures like this one where mercy has a companion. Like peanut butter and jelly go together, mercy goes hand-in-hand with other gifts from God. Mercy and something else—mercy and grace, mercy and longsuffering, or mercy and truth. What things go together with mercy? Who does mercy hang out with? If we were to flip a coin, one side—whether it's heads or tails does not matter—would be mercy.

But if we flipped it over, we would see one of mercy's companions.

What goes together with mercy? We find the first one in Psalms 23:6 which says, "Surely goodness and mercy. . . ." There it is. There is the first companion of mercy—goodness. Surely goodness and mercy shall follow me all the days of my life, and I will dwell in the house of the Lord forever. What goes good with mercy? Goodness goes good with mercy.

How merciful and good was God to David? The life of David was not only a great expression of mercy, but it also revealed God's goodness. God went and found a forgotten shepherd boy and chose him as a king. After David killed Goliath, he was greatly rewarded. God preserved David from Saul, and He gave him his own army of 400 mighty men.

Later, God preserved David from Absalom and gave him new friends that would come alongside him. God showed mercy to David by helping him to bring the Ark of the Covenant back to Jerusalem. When David sinned with Bathsheba and murdered her husband, Uriah the Hittite, God showed him mercy. But not only mercy; God's goodness brought forth the next king, Solomon, out of that relationship. God was merciful when David numbered the people. Time and time again, God was not only merciful to David, but he was also good.

If you've ever had a smile given to you, or received a heartfelt hug, or an "I love you;" if you've ever been given a gift, or have wealth, or have made an accomplishment in your life; if God has blessed you with a family or steadfast, loyal friends—all of those are expressions of God's goodness. Your position, titles, influence, opportunity, looks, gifts, possessions, status, and access are all a by-product of God's goodness. You don't really believe you are that smart—do you?

I'm here to tell you that Jesus is better than good. How is God so good? Because He promises me that He will never leave me nor forsake me. God promises me that He'll always love me and accept me and He wants me. No matter how many times I fail, no matter how often I mess up, whenever I do wrong, God still loves me. He still accepts me. And he's still willing to forgive me if I ask for it. God is always thinking about me. God is always looking out for my best interests and my best welfare. That is God's goodness to me—and it is the same for you.

The Bible says in Romans 8:28, "All things work together for good." God is good even when there is bad stuff in our lives. God is still good in the bad, tough, hard, difficult, painful, and sorrowful times. He finds a way to make all that work together for our advantage. It may not look great. It may not feel great. It may not sound great, but God gets involved in it and He turns it around to our good.

The book of Ephesians says, "Now unto him that is able to do exceeding abundantly above all that we ask or think" (Ephesians 3:20 KJV). God is good because He exceeds the dreams that we have. He does more than we can imagine. He outdoes our needs and wants and surpasses all our expectations. God's goodness is what we receive after failure, devastation, pain, or misery. Goodness is revealed in the times of laughter, joy, and merriment, where there was once sorrow and grief. Goodness is demonstrated in how far you have come—where you are today compared to where you once were. God is full of mercy and goodness. Wherever you see mercy you will see goodness there!

Mercy and God's Faithfulness

We find the second companion of mercy in the book of Lamentations, "Through the Lord's mercies we are not consumed, because His compassions fail not. They are new every morning; great is Your faithfulness" (Lamentations 3:22-23).

God's faithfulness—that God is absolutely reliable, God is absolutely dependable, and God is absolutely trustworthy—is the greatest, safest bet that you could ever make in your life. God was faithful to produce a promise for us after our mother and father, Adam and Eve, fell into sin. In the Garden He said there would come one from the womb of a woman that would bruise the heel of Satan. Then, Galatians 4:4 says that in the fullness of time, God sent forth His Son. That's a faithful promise through Jesus Christ, and He was faithful.

In 2 Chronicles 1:8, God promised David—He made a covenant with David—that he would always have an heir on the throne. Now some of those heirs were really bad kings, really perverted, and very immoral. But God was always faithful to that word. God was faithful to say, "David, you're making a covenant with me; I'm making a covenant with you. You will always have an heir."

Because God is faithful, we have confidence to pray. Because God is faithful, we have confidence when the devil is attacking us that he will be defeated. Because God is faithful, we have confidence that in the midst of temptation, God will give us strength. Because God is faithful, we know that when we're going through the most difficult time we can imagine that God will give us the courage to be faithful in that trial and that He will bring us through.

I have two dogs, Samson and Cocoa, a yellow lab and a chocolate lab. If there is one thing I can tell you about my dogs—they are faithful! When I go on a walk, they will not leave my side. When I'm in the house, they stay right there by the door. They are faithful, loyal companions to me, but they can't compare with the faithfulness of God.

When I was in the eighth grade there was a kid named Albert who was head and shoulders above every other kid. Perhaps you had a similar classmate in grade school—a kid with a deep voice that everybody literally had to look "up" to. Albert was already shaving and had a beard in the eighth grade. He looked like a man!

One day Albert and I got into an argument. We just disagreed on something, and Albert wanted to beat me up. Albert was big! But I played it off like I could fight, and I wasn't going to back down. But on the inside I was scared.

Well, I had a friend named Lucho who was about four years older than me. Lucho said, "Diego, if you ever need me, I'll be there." Now, we didn't have cell phones back then, so I ran to a pay phone. I'm dialing Lucho's number—ring, ring, ring, ring, ring—Lucho wasn't picking up! I was going to have to face Albert all by myself!

Have you ever had a friend like that who said they'd be there for you in your hour of need, but when you called on them, they weren't there? Thank God in our hour of need we can call upon Jesus and He is always faithful to pick up the phone, with no call waiting.

Mercy and Grace

The third companion of mercy is *grace*. Hebrews says this, "Let us therefore come boldly to the throne of grace, that we may obtain mercy and find grace to help in time of need" (Hebrews 4:16).

Abraham was merciful to Isaac, and he was gracious to Isaac. If you study the life of Abraham and go back to the point of Abraham's death, the Bible says that at the time of his death, Abraham had several children. He married a woman named Keturah after Sarah died (see Genesis 25:1), and he had several sons. And the Bible says he gave them gifts, but he gave all that he had to Isaac. That is a great picture of God's grace. Abraham gave all that he had to Isaac and that's what God does for us.

All of Abraham's sons received gifts from their father, but Isaac—as the favored, promised seed—received more than gifts. He received an inheritance, a heritage, a legacy, and all the rights and privileges associated with being the heir to the promise God had made to Abraham. God loves everyone and gives each person the gift of life and the many good things we receive here on Earth—even to those who do not accept Jesus as their Lord and Savior. But the child of God who accepts Jesus receives an inheritance in Christ—which is anything and everything that the Father is and has.

God is a God of mercy, but He's also a God of grace. Now let me tell you the difference, because many people don't know the difference between mercy and grace, and they will often use them interchangeably. Thank God for His grace. Thank God for His mercy. But you need to know there's a difference between grace and mercy.

For example, let me tell you what mercy does. Have you ever been pulled over by a policeman and you were guilty of some kind of traffic violation?

You know you got caught and you are in trouble—there is going to be a ticket given to you and a fine attached to it. Mercy is when the police officer says, "I'm not going to write you a ticket. I'm just going to give you a warning." That's mercy. He forgives you of your debt. He forgives you of your crime. With God, He forgives you of your sin, your wrongdoing—that's mercy.

So, what is grace? Here's what grace is—the policeman issues the ticket, but he takes the ticket and he pays the fine. That's grace extended toward you. So mercy and grace are companions that go hand-in-hand. Mercy forgives you, but grace blesses you. And that's what God did for you and me. Mercy is not getting what you deserve. It's deliverance from judgment. It's forgiving of a debt. It's cancelling a punishment. But grace is getting what you don't deserve. It's favor toward your unworthiness. It's blessing you even though you're guilty. It's a reward. It is favor in your life.

We have a little granddaughter, named Arielle. And this little girl is spoiled, especially by Cindy. She favors this girl. All Arielle has to do is look at something and Cindy will trip over it to get it for her. Right now this little girl is into dressing like princesses. So, within a short time Cindy has bought her a Cinderella dress, a Snow White dress, an Aurora dress, a Rapunzel dress, and a Tiana dress. I don't even know who these people are, but Arielle has all these princess dresses. And every day she comes out wearing a different one! Why? Because Cindy has favored her. She doesn't stop buying Arielle dresses—that child has more dresses than she can wear, and more princess dresses yet to come. Grace gives all. And that's what God has done for you. He favors you. He gives to you and He blesses you with things that you don't deserve and there are more blessings to come.

Mercy forgave you of your sin—but now look at what you have in your life. Whatever that looks like—family, love, relationships, influence, riches, prosperity, possessions—all those are pictures of God's mercy and grace.

Mercy and Justice

The fourth companion of mercy is justice or judgment. Psalms 101:1 says, "I will sing of mercy and justice; to You, O Lord, I will sing praises." A great picture of God's mercy and judgment is found in the story of Noah. God's mercy allowed Noah to preach to the unsaved heathen, lost, unbelievers for 120 years. "Give your heart to the Lord. God doesn't want to judge you, but it's going to rain. Everything is going to be wiped away." Punishment is coming. Consequences will happen!

Noah does that for 120 years! I could see 120 days or 120 months or maybe 12 years. But 120 years—that's the mercy of God. That's the forbearance of God. That's the longsuffering of God. But what happened after 120 years? Judgment comes. The flood came and life ended!

Another example is Sodom and Gomorrah. God allowed it to go on, and on, and on. We don't know exactly how long the people lived in defiance of God's Law through their acts of immorality and gross perversion, or how long He waited for them to repent. That time was evidence of God's mercy, but eventually judgment came. And so it is with God's mercy and God's judgment. The Bible mentions many times that God is slow to anger. But notice what it doesn't say—it doesn't say that He doesn't get angry. He's *slow* to anger. He doesn't get ticked off right away. He doesn't pronounce judgment right away. He doesn't rebuke you right away. He doesn't punish you right away. He doesn't send consequences right away. That's His mercy. He's slow to anger, but He does get angry.

A while ago I took a mini-cruise to Ensenada that left on Tuesday and came back on Saturday. So I had to put my sermon together on the cruise. Every once in a while I'd break away or get up really early and work on it. Well, I use the internet sometimes together with my Bible for whatever I'm researching. So I had to pay for wi-fi. I bought 200 minutes, thinking that would be plenty. But every time I logged on there was this clock that was ticking away. *Tick tick tick tick . . .* every *tick* was eating away at my time. And soon I started panicking, thinking, *I don't have enough time! I don't have enough time! I don't have enough time!* And sure enough, I ran out of time. I used up all of my 200 minutes. They vanished as quickly as my dogs devour their food. It was gone for good.

That's the way the world is living right now with the mercy of God. It's going like this...*tick tick tick tick.* Counting backwards. People aren't living right. They're not doing right. Fortunately, God is longsuffering. But the clock is ticking and eventually it's going to go to zero because mercy has to be connected to judgment. The end will eventually come and you don't want to be on the wrong side of the equation.

Some people try to use the mercy of God as a justification to sin and to ignore the judgment of God. How long will mercy last before they get busted; before they get caught; before they face consequences; before they reap what they sow; before there is a day of reckoning, retribution, retaliation, or payback?

We would not say someone should go on an endless charging spree when they don't have the money to pay for those charges. Or that we can afford to abuse our body endlessly without realizing that a day of reckoning will come. No. There's always a day of reckoning. Consequences will come for the choices we make. And so it is in the kingdom of God.

Now, the book of Luke tells the story of a certain fig tree, "He also spoke this parable: 'A certain man had a fig tree planted in his vineyard, and he came seeking fruit on it and found none. Then he said to the keeper of his vineyard, "Look, for three years I have come seeking fruit on this fig tree and find none. Cut it down; why does it use up the ground?" But he answered and said to him, "Sir, let it alone this year also, until I dig around it and fertilize it. And if it bears fruit, well. But if not, after that you can cut it down"'" (Luke 13:6-9).

Three years and no fruit. That's the mercy of God. But after four years, there is a day of reckoning. In Matthew 13:30, the Bible compares the kingdom of God to the tares and the wheat—those that believe in Jesus as their Lord, and those that don't. They grow together, but then there comes a time of harvest and then they will be separated. "Tares" are symbolic of unbelievers and "wheat" is symbolic of believers. They also represent an ungodly lifestyle compared with a godly one. People think, *I'm getting away with it. I can live wrong, and no consequences happen. I didn't get cancer. I didn't lose my job. My wife didn't find out.* But there's going to come a day when the wheat and the tares are exposed and separated. You cannot habitually practice sin.

Don't be fooled. "Do you not know that the unrighteous will not inherit the kingdom of God? Do not be deceived. Neither fornicators, nor idolaters, nor adulterers, nor homosexuals, nor sodomites, nor thieves, nor covetous, nor drunkards, nor revilers, nor extortioners will inherit the kingdom of God" (1 Corinthians 6:9-10). That's consequences.

This truth is reiterated in the book of Revelation. "But the cowardly, unbelieving, abominable, murderers, sexually immoral, sorcerers, idolaters, and all liars shall have their part in the lake which burns with fire and brimstone, which is the second death" (Revelation 21:8).

There are consequences. You can't just think that the Lord is going to forgive you if you don't repent, and if you don't change your lifestyle. No more lies, false gods, errors, deception, and compromise. Justice and judgment follow mercy.

Mercy and Truth

Psalm 25:10 says, "All the paths of the Lord are mercy and truth, to such as keep His covenant and His testimonies." *Truth* is the fifth companion of mercy. The truth that you believe, that Jesus died for you, forgave you, accepted you, and made you His righteousness.

In 1773, a man named John Newton wrote the lyrics for one of the most famous hymns in Christendom called *Amazing Grace.* At one time he was a slave trader who then got saved and became a pastor. And on his tombstone it reads, "Once an infidel and a libertine, a slave owner in Africa, but by the rich mercy of our Lord Jesus Christ was preserved, restored, and pardoned, appointed to preach the faith he had long labored to destroy"—what a picture of God's mercy.

In the first chapter of Matthew we read the genealogy of Jesus. It traces the family lineage, the bloodline that He came from. If you go back, you will read of four women—great, great, great-grandmothers of Jesus. All four of these women had a past. The first one that is mentioned is Tamar. The second one is Rahab. The third one is Ruth. The fourth one is Bathsheba.

Each of these women had a past that most would say disqualified them. A whore, a prostitute, an idol-worshipper, and an adulteress. That was truth; it cannot be denied. That's who they once were. But mercy came in and said, "You are forgiven. Your past is wiped away. When you acknowledge your sins, I will forget them—as far as the east is from the west" (Psalm 103:11, paraphrased). First John 1:9 says if you confess your sins, He is faithful and just to forgive you of your sins and to cleanse you from all unrighteousness.

Truth said that these women were guilty. Truth said that they should not be pardoned. But mercy said, "Acquitted, clemency, and innocent." That's the amazing thing that mercy overrides the truth, the reality, of what we once were. God's mercy is able to deny what did happen, because of Jesus.

Second Corinthians 5:21 says this, "He was made to be sin who knew no sin, that we might be made the righteousness of God in Christ Jesus" (paraphrased). You're not *trying* to be righteous; you *are* righteous. Your DNA and your character and your nature is now righteous. Jesus is righteous, so when you accepted Jesus Christ, His righteousness came upon you. Truth acknowledges facts and reality. Mercy doesn't ignore truth, but instead steps in and redefines that truth with a new existence, outcome, and result.

Mercy and Hope

The sixth companion of mercy is *hope*. Mercy and hope. "Behold, the eye of the Lord is on those who fear Him, on those who hope in His mercy" (Psalm 33:18). Mercy gives us a reason to hope.

Do you remember the story of the prodigal son in Luke chapter 15? The prodigal said, "I'm going to return home, and I'm going to beg for mercy. And I'm going to acknowledge the sin in my life." It was the hope that his father would give him mercy that allowed him to return.

Mercy is God's loving kindness as seen through his compassion, pity, sympathy, forgiveness, forbearance, and generosity. All of these are a great practice of the inexhaustible mercy that was shown to the prodigal son in Luke 15.

Notice the father's disposition is not to judge, but to rescue the prodigal son or daughter—which we all once were or presently are. There is a difference between condemning someone—giving the opinion that they are hopeless and without the capability to change—casting judgment and wrath, or separating ourselves from others with the idea that we are better. It does not have to do with how we see people and what we feel inside of our hearts towards people in their sin. We don't condemn, but we also don't condone. We can still speak the truth to people and share Jesus' love and forgiveness. We can still hold to our Bible-based convictions without hating people. We can show them love and friendship without having to be in agreement or acceptance of their sin.

Let's look at how mercy came in Luke 15:18, 21 "I will arise and go to my father, and will say to him, 'Father, I have sinned against heaven and before you' . . . and the son said to him, 'Father, I have sinned against heaven and in your sight, and am no longer worthy to be called your son.'"

The son participated in everything that money could buy. Anything that was in his heart to do. Nothing withheld and with no restraint. It was wild and illicit, filthy, lewd, perverted, and freaky. Would it make Hugh Hefner blush? The Bible says he joined himself to that lifestyle. He was getting wasted. He was enjoying it. But then he came to himself and said, "I want to change, I need help, I'm tired of this lifestyle" and his knowledge of his father's mercy drove him back home. He knew his father was merciful no matter how long or how bad he was. He humbled himself by letting go of his pride and began his journey home. His level of repentance activated and released the mercy in his father's heart.

Notice in Luke 15:20 that mercy, as represented by the father, was watching and waiting for him to return; ready, willing, and available to lavish mercy in all its expression and dimensions. Notice that mercy is full of compassion, love, pity, and sympathy. That means it identifies and relates. Mercy ran towards him—not a mosey, stroll, walk, or jog—but a full-on sprint with eagerness, energy, passion, excitement, and tears of joy. Then Mercy embraced him while he was still filthy, dirty, and nasty with the stench of his smelly clothes, which represents his sinful lifestyle.

Mercy was not afraid to touch him. Mercy kissed him, even with bad breath and all (and didn't ask him to first put a tic tac in his mouth). Mercy showered him with non-stop sloppy kisses like how a mama kisses her baby. It was a kiss of restoration which demonstrated the father's tenderness toward the son. He wanted this son to feel his love—a reflection of the all-encompassing acceptance, forgiveness and tender mercies of God's love. Mercy was generous to give him a robe of honor and respect to replace his rags, a ring of authority to reinstate him, sandals for a new direction, and a sonship position, not one as a slave. Mercy gave the once lost, far-from-God and from his purpose son the biggest and best party that could ever take place with the best food, entertainment, decorations, and location. All because of God's amazing mercy and His loving kindness.

Please understand that God is not mad at you. He wants to shower His mercy on any prodigal son or daughter who is repentant, broken, tired, empty, and willing to change the direction of their lives. No matter how long you were away from the Father or how long you've been doing something, God says "Come home prodigal son or daughter."

In the same way as the story of the Prodigal Son, mercy gives us hope in our lives. Mercy gives us hope to believe for a better future, to believe for change, that things are going to be different, that things are going to get better, and that we can have a confident assurance of expectation.

The lepers were given hope through mercy. Elijah was given hope through mercy. The woman caught in the very act of adultery was certainly given mercy, but Jesus' words to her also gave her hope. Blind Bartimaeus was given hope that Jesus would heal him. Peter denied the Lord three times, but mercy gave him a future through hope. When you begin to understand more about the mercy of God, hope begins to rise up in your heart. A belief that things can change begins to take root. Hope will convince you that there can be a different outcome that mercy wants to give you. And that's what God can do through us. Mercy and hope work together.

A scientific experiment was done with rats in a bathtub of water. The rats were put into the bathtub with just enough water so they could keep their nose above the water. They would swim for about two hours and then someone would pick them up and hold them for a while. Then they would put them back in the water for another two hours and this was repeated over and over again.

Then the bathtub was filled with water and another set of rats were put in and they swam for about two hours and then drowned. Then the first sets of rats were put in again and they swam and swam for 24 hours. The result of the experiment was this: the first group of rats were able to swim for 24 hours because they were conditioned to have hope that someone would lift them up out of the water and hold them so they kept on kicking. What does that say to you?

First Thessalonians 4:13 says this, "But I do not want you to be ignorant, brethren, concerning those who have fallen asleep, lest you sorrow as others who have no hope." The mercy of God forgave me of my sins, and now I hope. I have a hope that I'm going to go to Heaven; that when I fall asleep and I die, I'm not just going into an eternal rest. I'm going on to glory. I'm going on to Heaven. That's my blessed hope—Jesus Christ.

Mercy and Righteousness

The last companion to mercy is found in Proverbs 21:21, "He who follows righteousness and mercy, finds life, righteousness, and honor." The seventh companion to mercy is righteousness. What does that mean? Somebody could say, "You know what? I'm very merciful toward people." But that doesn't mean that you are righteous or living a righteous life. You are in right-standing with God if you're a Christian, but that may not mean that you're living a righteous life before God through your acts, deeds, lifestyle, conversation, attitudes, and behaviors. You might be postionally righteous, but not functioning righteously.

God doesn't just want us to be merciful toward one another, "Well, I forgive you for what you've done." He expects us to live holy and to live right. He doesn't want us to be 80-proof Christians, or 66-proof Christians. He wants us to be 100-proof Christians. When God extends mercy toward you, it not only offers you forgiveness, but it brings its companion of righteousness with it. Righteousness— the ability to love, serve, and obey God; the ability to please Him; the ability to have victory over temptation and sin.

Have you ever met somebody who takes pictures and says, "You know what? I have a good side, and I have a bad side. Please get me on my good side." Cindy is that way. She thinks that she has a good side. Well, to me both sides are good, but in her mind for some reason—I don't know if her hair falls a certain way, or she thinks the angle of her cheekbone is best, or . . . I don't know what she's thinking—but if you ever see a picture of us, you'll notice she's always on the left side of me. She will never be on the right because she thinks that's not her good side.

As you live for God right now, make sure that you have two good sides. "God, I just want you to see my good side." No, God wants you to be a 360-degree Christian—all areas of your life. No posing allowed. Not only when you are in church, but also when you are at work and when you are at home. Not only when you are in front of Christians, but also when you are in front of sinners. That is what righteousness looks like. Not just when you're around certain people, but in all environments and in every aspect of your life.

There are people who are ambidextrous, meaning they have the same strength in both hands, both arms, and both legs—one is not weaker than the other. Most of us are dominant on one side. You're either a "righty" or a "lefty" and your other side is weaker. But if you are ambidextrous, then you are strong on both sides.

God wants us to be ambidextrous Christians. Not just strong in one area—but in every area of our lives. Not just strong in faith, but strong in giving; not just strong in your prayer life, but strong in forgiving other people. Strong in our character, integrity, and lifestyles. These are the companions of mercy. I love these companions, and I hope that you will become enamored with them, too.

☩ Questions for Reflection

What does God's goodness look like to you?

_____

_____

_____

Where has God been faithful to you?

_____

_____

_____

Where has God shown grace to you?

_____

_____

_____

What does time running out mean to you?

_____

_____

_____

How do you relate to the story of the prodigal?

_____

_____

_____

What does righteousness mean to you?

_____

_____

_____

Questions for Life Changes

Where can I change?

_____

_____

_____

What can I change?

_____

_____

_____

When can I change?

_____

_____

_____

How can I change?

_____

_____

_____

Who can I change?

_____

_____

_____

Questions for Group Study

Can you name the companion of mercy?

_____

_____

_____

Who was God good to in the Bible showing mercy and why?

_____

_____

_____

Where in the Bible has God shown faithfulness and why?

_____

_____

_____

Who in the Bible experienced grace? What does this mean to you?

_____

_____

_____

What does justice with grace look like?

_____

_____

_____

When does time run out?

_____

_____

_____

What does righteousness and mercy look like?

_____

_____

_____

What does justice mean?

_____

_____

_____

What does hope mean?

_____

_____

_____

Where and how does the prodigal son receive mercy?

_____

_____

_____

CHAPTER 5

A Vessel of Mercy

In Genesis chapter 32 is an amazing story about a guy named Jacob. Jacob stole his brother's birthright, and because of that his twin brother, Esau, was going to kill him. So Jacob fled in terror and he went to his mama's people. He was really a mama's boy anyway. He ran away with nothing. He was in so much fear he didn't even take a change of clothes. He didn't take any cattle. He didn't take any coins. He didn't take any silver. He couldn't rub two nickels together.

Eventually he becomes the richest man on the planet with more cattle and land than anyone else and with many servants and possessions. And as he looks back over his life, he says, "I am not worthy of the least of all the mercy and loving-kindness and all the faithfulness which You have shown to Your servant, for with [only] my staff I passed over this Jordan [long ago], and now I have become two companies" (Genesis 32:10 AMP). Jacob calls God's blessing in his life an act of God's mercy. "For with only my staff. . . ."

Can you remember a day when you had nothing—before your title, before your position, before your wealth, before your property—when dinner was a cup of ramen noodles, your old used car broke down all the time, or maybe you didn't even have a car and had to take the bus? Do you remember what you once were? Can you look back like Jacob and say, "I was nothing? I didn't have anything. And now I've become something, but it's all because of the mercy of God."

Because of God's mercy to us, we need to live in constant awareness and recognition of what great mercies He has given to us; that we've come from nothing to something. It is a reminder of the truth that if you are faithful to God, serve Him, and look toward His mercy—no matter how little you begin with, look at where your life can end. You can have everything. The world has nothing to offer you. The devil will claim to offer you everything, but will steal, kill, and destroy your life. But the Bible says, "The blessing of the Lord, it maketh rich, and he addeth no sorrow with it" (Proverbs 10:22 KJV).

David said, "I'm old, but I was young, and I've never seen the righteous forsaken, nor his seed begging bread" (Psalm 37:25, paraphrased). I've been serving God since I was 17 years old. I look back at my life and I have no regrets that I gave God my teens, my 20s, my 30s, my 40s, and now my 50s! God has blessed my life richly!

Mercy is God's extraordinary and uncommon goodness. It is His willingness to pardon us rather than to punish us. There are many, many things that mercy goes with. We love the word *mercy* in our labels, titles, names, and vocabulary. There are mercy hospitals. There are mercy ships. There are mercy rules. There are mercy angels, mercy organizations, and mercy clubs.

There is a story about a collector who spent $14,000 on a decorative egg, but before long he started to regret his impulse buy. He was sure he had overspent for this egg. But he held onto it for about 10 years, and then decided he was going to go scrap it for the value of the metal. He estimated that he could get about $5,000, and he would take the

$9,000 loss. But then he started to research what this egg was, and he found out that it was a Faberge egg made for the Czar of Russia in 1887 and worth 33 million dollars.

That's a great illustration of how many of us view mercy. We don't value mercy. We almost want to scrap it away. And we don't realize what it is worth. And yet, Ephesians 2:4 talks about how God is rich in mercy toward us because of His great love.

The greatest expression and demonstration of mercy is Jesus dying for us. For a Christian, every day is resurrection day and when we say the word *mercy*, we ought to think about Jesus. When you think about mercy, you ought to think about the cross; about how God's love toward us took our place on that cross.

There's a story about Robert the Bruce, the soon-to-be king of Scotland, who was being hounded and chased by the English who wanted to kill him. They didn't want him to come to power because they saw him as a threat. So they got the bloodhounds that he used to go hunting with, because they were so familiar with Robert the Bruce's scent, and they ran him across the countryside. They wearied him. They wore him down. He was almost at the end of his strength and his soldiers said, "They're going to catch us. Let's give up." But he said, "No, not yet. I've got one more strategy."

And he ran into a river and he walked in that river for miles. When the bloodhounds reached the river, his scent had been washed away by the water and so they were unable to track him any farther. So Robert the Bruce avoided capture and went on to become king.

That is a great picture of what Jesus did for us. As the enemy was hunting us down, hounding and wearying us, and wearing us out with our sinful lifestyle and our deviant rebellion, we couldn't shake the enemy. We couldn't shake the sin. We couldn't shake the alcoholism, the bitterness, the jealousy, and the unforgiveness. But then we walked through the river of Jesus' blood and it cleansed us. Now the enemy has no victory over us to hound us anymore.

The Responsibility for Mercy

We've laid the foundation of the truth that we are recipients of God's mercy and how great God's mercy is toward us. But we have a responsibility, too. So many Christians don't like the word *respon-sibility*. We think we can be a Christian and avoid responsibility. Why? Every family has responsibilities; every student, athlete, and leader. Why not the Christian? Where did the notion that accepting and believing in Jesus was all we had to do?

No, because of His mercy to me, I want to—*I get to*—serve Him and obey Him. If I've partaken of the cup or the well of mercy, am I not obligated to give that mercy to someone else? The truth is we've not just sipped on God's mercy—we've drunk pints, quarts, and gallons of it. But for so many of us, we will only offer someone else a "sip." Because when you offend me, mistreat me, abuse me, insult me, and talk about me, I'm not sure I want to give you any of the mercy that I've been drinking by the gallon.

When I missed it, when I cried out, when I royally messed up and pleaded, "God, forgive me!" I desperately wanted those gallons of mercy that He poured on me, but now when someone walks down that same road I was on and offends me, I'm not sure that I'm even concerned about what they want or need. I tend to want to put people on rations, quotas, and reserves when it comes to mercy. We often want a different distribution rate—more for us, less for them! But mercy is endless, bountiful, and limitless.

We often think of mercy as being only vertical—flowing from God to us. But when we personally receive something from Jesus, it isn't just vertical, it's also intended to be horizontal—something we receive to give to others. We are recipients, but we are to then become distributors; sharers; allocators of God's mercy. Too many people have become consumers only. They keep mercy for themselves instead of being a distributor.

What is our responsibility? The Bible says, "That He might make known the riches of His glory on the vessels of mercy, which He had prepared before-hand for glory" (Romans 9:23). Notice that God calls us, "vessels of mercy." Is that what you are to your neighbor, family, and even strangers? When your boss chews you out or a co-worker steals your promotion, are you a vessel of mercy? When that family member takes something of yours, are you a vessel of mercy? Is that how you see yourself—as a conduit, as a channel for the mercy of God? Well, you are a vessel whether you give it out or not, but most of us are plugged up, clogged up, and stopped up. It comes easy to us to be vessels of wrath, rage, and hatred; getting even with people; doing unto others the way they have hurt us, mistreated us, and disappointed us. But vessels of mercy?

Abraham Lincoln said, "I have always found that mercy bears richer fruit than strict justice." We are called to be vessels of mercy to hurting humanity, to people who don't deserve it. Mercy is supposed to flow through us freely to anyone that needs it.

The second thing we are to be is this: "He who exhorts, in exhortation; he who gives, with liberality; he who leads, with diligence; he who shows mercy, with cheerfulness" (Romans 12:8). The Apostle Paul is talking about gifts bestowed upon the body of Christ. We need to recognize that mercy is a gift that you and I are called to give to people who don't deserve it. It's a donation; it's a present for someone else.

The best gifts are free gifts, generous gifts, and overwhelming gifts. And that's the gift of mercy that you need to give people. You need to surprise people with the gift of mercy. Natural gifts are soon forgotten, lost, or worn out, but mercies are unforgettable, always in season, always acceptable. Have you ever given a gift to someone and you were so excited to see their reaction? You were probably anticipating how they would feel—hopefully surprised and overwhelmed. Sometimes I buy my wife, Cindy, gifts for her birthday, our anniversary, or Christmas, but I simply can't wait for the holiday to come and so I give it to her before the official day because I'm so excited. Mercy can be that same kind of gift, but it doesn't require money, wrapping, or going into debt. Just a helping hand, a kind heart, a warm smile, the love of Christ. You are a vessel of mercy—a gift of mercy to someone.

The third thing God expects of us is found in Micah 6:8, "He has shown you, O man, what is good. And what does the Lord require of you but to do justly, to love mercy, and to walk humbly with your God?" Everyone wants a definition of what is good. Everyone asks, "What does God require of me every day of my life?" In this passage from Micah, we have three things. But notice the middle one that God requires of us—*to love mercy.*

Now, to be honest, I don't love giving mercy. Do you love giving mercy? When someone cuts you off on the freeway do you say, "Oh, I just love to give you mercy!" Is that what comes out of you? When your wife is chewing you out, is that what comes out of you—*I love to give you mercy*? What about when someone makes fun of you? Or when your next-door neighbor does something mean? Probably not. But we've got to work toward this because God requires it. In essence, we are obligated. We are ordered by God to give mercy to people. It is required.

Now, don't take this thought to the extreme that you believe you should have to take abuse or suffer personal attacks. But when someone takes the parking space that you've been waiting for at the crowded mall at Christmas, does "joy to the world" or "Merry Christmas!" come out of your mouth? Or something else?

God expects us to give mercy, which means it needs to be available. It needs to be accessible, and it really needs to be obtainable in someone's life so that they can receive the mercy that you have to give them. Again, what is mercy? Forbearance, longsuffering, extraordinary and uncommon goodness, compassion, sympathy—they should be able to expect that from you.

Have you ever had to go to the bathroom really bad, and you went into a store and asked, "Can I use your restroom?"

And they said, "No. This is for employees only."

And you pleaded, "You know, I really got to go bad!"

"No. For employees only."

"Listen, I'll buy something in a minute. Can I go?"

"No!"

Believe me, the people in these places deal with this all the time, and mercy is rarely the response they give. Like God's mercy, it has become a rare, if not extinct, event in our society today. That makes it even more important that we make sure that mercy is accessible and available to people. Not like a gas station or store that says "for employees only."

Four Reasons Why

Now maybe you are wondering, *Well, why do I have to be merciful when people mistreat me, when they abuse me, when they insult me, when they talk about me, and when they hurt me? Why do I have to be merciful? You don't know what they have done to me.*

I am so glad you asked these difficult questions, because the Bible has an answer—it always does. Matthew 5:7 says, "Blessed are the merciful, for they shall obtain mercy." Read that over and over and let it sink into your heart.

I don't know of anyone who doesn't want to be blessed. You even hear people that aren't saved or don't go to church use the word "blessed." I'm blessed. I'm blessed. I'm blessed. Do you want to be blessed? Do you want more blessings in your life? Do you want to remain blessed? Then you have to be merciful.

God said, "I'm going to royally bless you." What is blessing? Favor, promotion, increase, prosperity, provision, protection, good fortune, happiness—everything that mankind yearns for. What is it connected to? Listen, people want to be happy today. You don't know how many people are lonely. You don't know how many people in this world are depressed. You don't know how many people in this world are royally angry. You don't know how many people in this world walk in fear. What do they all want? They want happiness. And God says, "I've got happiness for you. Start being a merciful person and you'll start being happy and really blessed."

Could that be why so many Christians are depressed? Maybe they are depressed because they won't forgive their ex-husband or their ex-wife. They won't forgive their parents. They won't forgive their boss. They won't forgive their ex-pastor or current pastor. But God promises, "I'm going to bless your life if you'll be merciful to someone who doesn't deserve it."

The next thing Jesus says in Luke is this, "Therefore be merciful, just as your Father also is merciful" (Luke 6:36). Why do we need to be merciful? Because we want to be like our Father. Isn't that what Christianity is all about? Isn't that why we gave our lives to Jesus—so that we could be more like Him? Isn't that what the title "Christian" means—to be Christ-like in our lives? Or is it just a religious title? Christianity is not a belief. It is a behavior.

Why am I going to be merciful? Because my Father is merciful, and I want to be like my Father—not like my former father, the devil, who the Bible talks about. I know how to be that kind of son to that father—mean, selfish, hateful, malicious, rude, cruel, and a person full of retaliation. *I'm gonna get even! You better not mess with me! You don't know who you're talking to!* That comes easy, being the child of that father. But can you be a child of the real Father?

So He says this . . . He doesn't tell you to copy the mercy of your mama, or copy the mercy of your natural daddy, or copy the mercy of your pastor, or copy the mercy of the elders in the church. He says, "I want you to copy My mercy—the mercy I demonstrated when I hung on that cross and those people mocked Me, spit on Me, crucified me, and abused Me. When everyone forsook Me, and yet I showed them love and mercy, that's what I expect you to do."

But, but, but. . . . No, no, that's what He told you, "Act like Me." Act like your Father.

You know, every father who has a son, and I imagine mothers who have a daughter can identify, but every father who has a son gets to a point where that young boy tries on his clothes, whether it's his shoes, his pants, his jacket, or his hat and he says, "Look at me, Daddy! I'm just like you!" And it warms the heart of the father that his son wants to be like him. One of my favorite pictures on my desk at work is a picture of my oldest son, Nathan, wearing my suit jacket when it was so big on him that it touched the floor. He wanted to look like, or resemble, his daddy. I can't help but think that it warms the heart of the Father God to say, "My child wants to be like Me. My child is like me in every way."

There was a time in the mid-70s when *Saturday Night Fever* was out, and I wanted to be like John Travolta. I wanted to dance like him, and I wanted that off-white outfit and platform shoes—so I could be the disco king. And my mom and I went all over L.A. looking for it. She'd say, "Here it is, Diego."

And I'd say, "No, that's not it."

"Here it is."

"No, that's not it." I knew what it looked like in my mind, and I wasn't going to settle for anything less or something that *almost* looked like the off-white suit with the platform shoes. I wanted to be just like John Travolta.

Finally we found it. When we got home I hung the suit up and just looked at it. I could see myself walking real cool like the disco king and making the moves on the dance floor like him. But after a few seconds it dawned on me, that I didn't dance, nor could I do the John Travolta moves.

The truth is we should want to be just like our Father and copy, imitate, and mimic Him. And the way we can be just like our Father is to be merciful to people who don't deserve mercy. They deserve retaliation. They deserve for us to get even. They deserve to be hurt. They deserve to die. They deserve for us to be cold-blooded, cold-hearted toward them.

Why mercy? Here's the third reason: "The merciful man does good for his own soul, but he who is cruel troubles his own flesh" (Proverbs 11:17).

Wow! *You mean, when I don't show someone mercy I hurt myself?* You got it!

Do you want trouble in your life? Do you want bad things? Do you want to hurt yourself? Then don't be merciful to anyone. I don't wake up in the morning saying "Today, I want to hit my thumb with a hammer," or "I want to hit my head on something," or "I want to stub my toe so I can feel pain and hurt." I don't know about you, but I want what is good for my soul and body—and I get that when I am merciful. I don't want to hurt myself. And it's unhealthy for me not to be merciful because then it allows rage, cold-heartedness, insensitivity, and unresponsiveness to take root in me.

You know the story of Job—he lost his children. He lost his wealth. He has boils, and he's full of sickness. And he has three friends that are so-called "comforters" who come to help him. But in fact, they judge him and say, "There's sin in your life. It's the wrath of God. You must be doing something wrong."

But Job makes this statement in Job 16:2, "I have heard many such things; miserable comforters are you all!"

Have you ever had friends like that—just plain miserable? I remember when I was fighting cancer, a member of our church came up to me and said, "Pastor, you don't look good. You need to go home."

I felt like saying, "Miserable comforter are you." But I couldn't, because I am a pastor.

But Job makes this amazing statement. He says this in verse three, "Shall words of wind have an end? Or what provokes you that you answer? I also could speak as you *do*, if your soul were in my soul's place. I could heap up words against you, and shake my head at you" (Job 16:3-4).

Essentially, Job is saying, "If the role was reversed. . . ." And that's what you need to tell yourself when you don't want to be merciful to someone. What if the shoe was on the other foot? Because one day it's going to be on the other foot. Do you know that you're going to mess up one day? You're going to say something you shouldn't say. You're going to think something you shouldn't think. We need to recognize that God would never require us to give mercy if we hadn't first asked for it and received mercy. He wouldn't require us to sow mercy if we hadn't first reaped mercy. And somehow I think God keeps a record of how much mercy we've taken in over our lifetime. Think of it this way—God will only require you to give mercy in the amount you have received from Him. So if you have never been a recipient, you don't have to deliver!

There was a man serving a six-year prison sentence, and he was about ready to be released. For six years he had been haunted by the memory of someone who had done him wrong before he went into prison. In fact, this guy threw a rock, a boulder, on his head, knocked him out, and stole $60 from his pocket. He was enraged. He said, "When I get out, I'm going to get even." He couldn't wait to get out. He was already plotting and planning what he was going to do.

With only a few days left before he was to get out, he got a new roommate in prison, and guess who the roommate was? Yep, the guy who had hit him over the head and stole the $60! He could hardly believe it—and he was boiling!

Now the guy that hit him over the head didn't recognize who he was. And the new prisoner knew that the old prisoner was going to be released in a couple of days, and he had the audacity to say, "You know, you're going to be released in a couple of days. Can I have your boots before you go?"

And the man thought, *Yeah, I'm going to give you my boots, but you're not going to like where I'm going to put them!*

But it just so happened that the prisoner who was about to be released had started going to chapel. He was watching videos and was hearing about the mercy of God and the forgiveness that God bestowed upon us for our debt and our sin. Something rose up in him that amazed him. A few days later, he was released in the middle of the night. And when the man's roommate woke up, he found the man's boots sitting right by his head.

Extending mercy to others does us good. That man's body would have been free from prison because he served his time, but he would never have been freed in his heart if he had chosen to hold on to his anger and resentment. And there are a lot of people who drive around in nice cars and have nice homes, who will never go into an actual prison cell, but they are bound the entire time by what has happened in the past. I have often wondered if God doesn't set these moments up where we encounter people who have hurt us and stolen from us in the past to give us an opportunity not only to show mercy, but also get healed! All too often, we think they are merely chance meetings or coincidences.

The fourth reason why we must show mercy is found in 2 Samuel 22:26. He says this, "With the merciful You will show Yourself merciful; with the blameless man You will show Yourself blameless."

This verse is saying if you sow mercy, you will reap mercy. The idea is what you give, you get. What you sow, you get in return. People that don't even know God have this rule that says, "What goes around comes around." They live by that rule. They talk about "karma," but they don't have the faintest idea that it was written thousands of years ago: "Whatsoever a man soweth, that shall he also reap" (Galatians 6:7 KJV).

Now, I can't guarantee that if you sow mercy into someone's life, you're going to reap mercy from them because some people don't reciprocate what has been given to them. But God says, "I'll remember." God accrues an account on your behalf.

Not long ago I got a certificate in the mail to REI (Recreational Equipment, Inc.). I shop at REI every once in a while—it's an outdoor sports shop—and every time I buy something, I accrue dividends or credits.

So I decide to go shopping because I had accrued $150. I'm walking around there like a big shot thinking, "What am I going to spend my money on?" I'm like a little kid! Picking up this and picking up that, "Nah, I don't want that!" And trying this on, "Nah, I don't want that!" So finally, I bought a pair of glasses for me to use when I bike for $60. I bought a new pair of earphones and a pair of swim goggles for the summer. I walked out of the store with all that stuff for free—because I had accrued something in my account.

What have you accrued in your mercy account?

Think about this: why was God so merciful to David? David really didn't deserve God's mercy. If someone murders, do you think they deserve mercy? What if your best friend commits adultery with your mate, and then when your back's turned, he kills you. And then he lies about it. Do you think he deserves mercy?

Then why is God so merciful to this man called David? He never takes his throne away from him and continues to bless him. We know David had a heart after God—but I think one of the reasons was because he sowed mercy. He sowed mercy to Saul, his father-in-law who tried to murder him, by sparing Saul's life. He sowed mercy to Absalom, his own son that tried to take his throne, by not hurting him. He sowed mercy to Mephibosheth, grandson to

Saul and son of Jonathan, even though kings murdered descendants of previous rulers to cut off the line of succession. He showed mercy to Shimei who cussed him out, following him along the road. He showed mercy to Nabal, the fool who forgot about David's generosity during his own prosperity. His life was full of episodes of mercy, and I think because of that he had accrued plenty of mercy in his account. So when it was needed, God could look back and say, "You've been merciful."

How do we build a mercy account? "For as the heavens are high above the earth, so great is His mercy toward those who fear Him" (Psalm 103:11). To fear God means you reverence God, honor God, and obey God. When you do these things, you accrue mercy to your account.

In Psalms it says, "But I have trusted in Your mercy; my heart shall rejoice in Your salvation" (Psalm 13:5). Trust God and it builds mercy. Trust God and it accrues mercy. Mercy is something you can fully rely on, depend upon, and put your confidence in. Unfortunately, we often have more trust in a vending machine to give us what we want than God.

Next, we must pray for people. Pray that God would be merciful to someone—the same way

Abraham prayed for Sodom and Gomorrah; the same way as the man in Luke 13 who had a vineyard came and said to the owner, "Tear down that tree because after three years, it's not producing." The steward then said, "Give it one more year." That's intercession. That's prayer. Pray to God for people in your family, your neighbors, and your friends that need God's mercy.

In James 2:13 it says, "Mercy triumphs over judgment." Can people take advantage of your mercy? The answer is absolutely yes! But isn't that what you want? It's a play on words. So, yes, people are going to take advantage of your mercy. But if I'm going to err, I'd rather err on the side of mercy than justice. And that's what James 2:13 talks about, "Mercy triumphs over judgment."

Can we be merciful and still demand consequences? Is it possible to be a Christian who forgives someone, has compassion and sympathy, but also must make a tough choice? Absolutely. Many Christians struggle with this. They will ask, "I forgive this person, but do I have to trust them again?" The answer is no. You can show someone mercy, but that doesn't mean you have to trust them. You can show someone mercy, but that doesn't mean you have to be financially generous to them again. You can show mercy to them, but that doesn't mean you have to repeat something you did with them again. You can show someone mercy, but that doesn't mean you have to give them another opportunity. You can show someone mercy, but that doesn't mean you don't have to fire them. You can show someone mercy, but that doesn't mean you have to stay married to them.

Let me explain. How do you judge the consequences of a spouse? Number one, you better have prayed and heard God. Number two, they had better have violated scripture and you have scriptural backing. When are consequences OK? When this person continues to repeat the offense or when you are fearful for your life because you are being threatened. Now God hates divorce, but staying married to somebody who is threatening your life—that's stupidity. Mercy given to someone is unearned by them. You are obligated to give mercy, but trust in a relationship must be earned. There is a price.

There are consequences when an individual is hurting someone or can injure someone else. For example, if you have an older child who is on drugs all the time and is putting you or a younger sibling in danger. You can be merciful: "I'm sympathetic to you and I will try to get you help, but now there are consequences." You can tell them they have to get out of the house because you have to watch over this five-year-old and make sure they are safe.

When are people unmerciful? Well, Jonah was unmerciful toward the Ninevites. Jonah was a recipient of God's mercy, but he didn't want to be a demonstrator of God's mercy. See, there's a lot of "warehouse" Christians and not "distribution" Christians. They want to hold all the stockpiles, pallets of mercy, and never want to give it out. But we are called to be a distribution center.

Where are people unmerciful? They're often unmerciful in the areas that they struggle with most in their own life. They think, *You shouldn't be doing that! God's going to judge you!* because they're doing it themselves. We have all heard of preachers who have boldly talked about deviant lifestyles, only to later find out that they have been living a double life and have fallen prey to the same sin themselves. On the other hand, many people are unmerciful toward things that they have never struggled with themselves. Why? Because they haven't developed compassion through their own experiences.

The good news is that mercy is not based on what someone else does, but it's based on what

Jesus did for you. Being a vessel of mercy is your decision to be like Jesus to someone else—regardless of who they are or what they have done. So let us pour and pour and keep on pouring out mercy on everyone around us.

I hope you are overwhelmed by God's mercy of love that He has toward you. He loves you so much more than any man or woman could love you. If you have realized your need to repent and receive the mercy God has for you, say this prayer:

Dear Jesus,

I'm like the Prodigal Son. I need your mercy, forgiveness, and love. I have sinned and broken your laws, and I need to be cleansed and given a new life. So I come to you today just as I am in all my dirty clothes, tired, empty, lonely, and hurting. I receive Jesus as my Lord and Savior. Jesus, You died for me on the cross and right now I receive your forgiveness, love, and mercy. Today, I am forgiven, cleansed, and accepted. I am a child of God and a recipient of God's mercy.

In Jesus name,

Amen.

I pray that the understanding of mercy draws you closer to God and closer to people as you give it out. I pray that the mercy of God allows you to be healed, whole, and complete. I pray that every day you will wake up thanking God for His new mercy for that day and go to bed thanking Him for the mercies that kept you as you partook of that day. I pray the next time you hear the word "mercy" it will get your attention and capture your heart. I pray the next time you see misery in the world or in someone else's life you will pray the mercy of God over it or them. I pray the next time you experience the mercy of God in your life you will stop and reflect on just what has happened or could have happened! I pray that you understand that there is nothing you've done or could do that mercy will not reach out and forgive you for. I pray that you understand that God never wakes up on the wrong side of the bed, for He is always merciful.

Lastly, I pray that you understand that your God is a merciful Father—kind, generous, longsuffering, good, loving, forgiving, tender, compassionate, rich, abundant, full, and plenteous in mercy. Enjoy it!

✝ Questions for Reflection

Can you think of people you have been a vessel of mercy toward? What happened?

_____

_____

_____

Who are some people you can extend mercy toward? How?

_____

_____

_____

Do you tend to give more or receive more mercy? Why?

_____

_____

_____

Matthew 5:7 says "Blessed are the merciful, for they shall obtain mercy." What does that mean to you?

_____

_____

_____

Where can you act or move like God?

_____

_____

_____

_____

Can you think of someone that you have run into that needed your mercy? What did you do?

_____

_____

_____

_____

Can you think of times where you have been quick to judge? What happened?

_____

_____

_____

_____

Can you recall a situation where both mercy and consequences were extended to someone?

_____

_____

_____

_____

🙏 Questions for Life Changes

Where can I change?

_____

_____

_____

What can I change?

_____

_____

_____

When can I change?

_____

_____

_____

How can I change?

_____

_____

_____

Who can I change?

_____

_____

_____

Questions for Group Study

What are vessels of mercy?

_____

_____

_____

What is the meaning of the story of Robert the Bruce, King of Scotland?

_____

_____

_____

What does vertical and horizontal mercy look like?

_____

_____

_____

What are the four reasons to be merciful to someone?

_____

_____

_____

Can you share a story of running into people that you had an ill feeling toward and what happened?

_____

_____

_____

Why was God so merciful to David?

_____

_____

_____

How has this book helped you?

_____

_____

_____

Mercy Scriptures

2 Samuel 24:14   English Standard Version (ESV)
Then David said to Gad, "I am in great distress. Let us fall into the hand of the LORD, for his mercy is great; but let me not fall into the hand of man."

Psalm 9:10   Amplified Bible (AMP)
And those who know Your name [who have experienced Your precious mercy] will put their confident trust in You, For You, O LORD, have not abandoned those who seek You.

Psalm 18:50   Amplified Bible (AMP)
He gives great triumphs to His king, And shows steadfast love *and* mercy to His anointed, To David and his descendants forever.

Psalm 23:6   King James Version (KJV)
Surely goodness and mercy shall follow me all the days of my life: and I will dwell in the house of the LORD for ever.

Psalm 40:11   New International Version (NIV)
Do not withhold your mercy from me, Lord; may your love and faithfulness always protect me.

Psalm 51:1-2   New International Version (NIV)
Have mercy on me, O God, according to your unfailing love; according to your great compassion blot out my transgressions. Wash away all my iniquity and cleanse me from my sin.

Psalm 86:5   Amplified Bible (AMP)
For You, O Lord, are good, and ready to forgive [our sins, sending them away, completely letting them go forever and ever]; And abundant in lovingkindness and overflowing in mercy to all those who call upon You.

Psalm 100:5   Amplified Bible (AMP)
For the Lord is good; His mercy and lovingkindness are everlasting, His faithfulness [endures] to all generations.

Psalm 103:1-5   The Message (MSG)
O my soul, bless GOD, From head to toe, I'll bless his holy name! O my soul, bless GOD, don't forget a single blessing! He forgives your sins—every one. He heals your diseases—every one. He redeems you from hell— saves your life! He crowns you with love and mercy—a paradise crown. He wraps you in goodness—beauty eternal. He renews your youth—you're always young in his presence.

Psalm 106:1   Amplified Bible (AMP)

Praise the LORD! (Hallelujah!) Oh give thanks to the LORD, for He is good; For His mercy *and* lovingkindness endure forever!

Psalm 130:1-2   New International Bible (NIV)

Out of the depths I cry to you, Lord; Lord, hear my voice. Let your ears be attentive to my cry for mercy.

Psalm 136:1   Amplified Bible (AMP)

Give thanks to the Lord, for He is good; For His lovingkindness (graciousness, mercy, compassion) endures forever.

Psalm 136:26   Amplified Bible (AMP)

Give thanks to the God of heaven, For His lovingkindness (graciousness, mercy, compassion) endures forever.

Proverbs 3:3   Amplified Bible (AMP)

Do not let mercy *and* kindness and truth leave you [instead let these qualities define you]; Bind them [securely] around your neck, Write them on the tablet of your heart.

Proverbs 16:6   Amplified Bible (AMP)

By mercy *and* lovingkindness and truth [not superficial ritual] wickedness is cleansed from the heart, And by the fear of the LORD one avoids evil.

Proverbs 28:13   New International Version (NIV)

Whoever conceals their sins does not prosper, but the one who confesses and renounces them finds mercy.

Micah 7:18   New International Version (NIV)

Who is a God like you, who pardons sin and forgives the transgression of the remnant of his inheritance? You do not stay angry forever but delight to show mercy.

Matthew 5:7   Amplified Bible (AMP)

"Blessed [content, sheltered by God's promises] are the merciful, for they will receive mercy.

Matthew 9:13   Amplified Bible, Classic Edition (AMPC)

Go and learn what this means: I desire mercy [that is, readiness to help those in trouble] and not sacrifice *and* sacrificial victims. For I came not to call *and* invite [to repentance] the righteous (those who are upright and in right standing with God), but sinners (the erring ones and all those not free from sin).

Matthew 9:13   New International Version (NIV)

But go and learn what this means: 'I desire mercy, not sacrifice.' For I have not come to call the righteous, but sinners."

Matthew 9:27   King James Version (KJV)

And when Jesus departed thence, two blind men followed him, crying, and saying, Thou son of David, have mercy on us.

Matthew 17:15   King James Version (KJV)

Lord, have mercy on my son: for he is lunatick, and sore vexed: for ofttimes he falleth into the fire, and oft into the water.

Matthew 20:30   King James Version (KJV)

And, behold, two blind men sitting by the way side, when they heard that Jesus passed by, cried out, saying, Have mercy on us, O Lord, thou son of David.

Mark 10:46-47   King James Version (KJV)

blind Bartimaeus, the son of Timaeus, sat by the highway side begging. And when he heard that it was Jesus of Nazareth, he began to cry out, and say, Jesus, thou son of David, have mercy on me.

Luke 1:50   Amplified Bible (AMP)

"And His mercy is upon generation after generation Toward those who [stand in great awe of God and] fear Him. from generation to generation.

Luke 1:77-79   New Living Translation (NLT)
You will tell his people how to find salvation through
forgiveness of their sins. Because of God's tender
mercy, the morning light from heaven is about to break
upon us, to give light to those who sit in darkness and in
the shadow of death, and to guide us to the path of peace."

Luke 17:12-13   King James Version (KJV)
And as he entered into a certain village, there met him
ten men that were lepers, which stood afar off: And they
lifted up their voices, and said, Jesus, Master, have
mercy on us.

Romans 3:23-24   Amplified Bible, Classic Edition (AMPC)
Since all have sinned and are falling short of the
honor *and* glory which God bestows *and* receives. [All]
are justified *and* made upright *and* in right standing with
God, freely *and* gratuitously by His grace (His unmerited
favor and mercy), through the redemption which is
[provided] in Christ Jesus,

Romans 6:14   Amplified Bible (AMP)
For sin will no longer be a master over you, since you are
not under Law [as slaves], but under [unmerited] grace
[as recipients of God's favor and mercy].

Romans 12:1   New International Version (NIV)
Therefore, I urge you, brothers and sisters, in view of
God's mercy, to offer your bodies as a living sacrifice,

holy and pleasing to God—this is your true and proper worship

1 Corinthians 16:23   Amplified Bible (AMP)
The grace of our Lord Jesus [His unmerited favor, His spiritual blessing, His profound mercy] be with you.

2 Corinthians 12:9   Amplified Bible (AMP)
but He has said to me, "My grace is sufficient for you [My lovingkindness and My mercy are more than enough—always available—regardless of the situation]; for [My] power is being perfected [and is completed and shows itself most effectively] in [your] weakness."Therefore, I will all the more gladly boast in my weaknesses, so that the power of Christ [may completely enfold me and] may dwell in me.

Ephesians 2:4   Amplified Bible, Classic Edition (AMPC)
But God—so rich is He in His mercy! Because of *and* in order to satisfy the great *and* wonderful *and* intense love with which He loved us,

1 Timothy 1:15-16   The Message (MSG)
Here's a word you can take to heart and depend on: Jesus Christ came into the world to save sinners. I'm proof—Public Sinner Number One—of someone who could never have made it apart from sheer mercy. And now he shows me off—evidence of his endless

patience—to those who are right on the edge of trusting him forever.

Titus 3:3-5   New Living Translation (NLT)

Once we, too, were foolish and disobedient. We were misled and became slaves to many lusts and pleasures. Our lives were full of evil and envy, and we hated each other. But— When God our Savior revealed his kindness and love, he saved us, not because of the righteous things we had done, but because of his mercy. He washed away our sins, giving us a new birth and new life through the Holy Spirit.

Hebrews 4:14-16   The Message (MSG)

Now that we know what we have—Jesus, this great High Priest with ready access to God—let's not let it slip through our fingers. We don't have a priest who is out of touch with our reality. He's been through weakness and testing, experienced it all—all but the sin. So let's walk right up to him and get what he is so ready to give. Take the mercy, accept the help.

Hebrews 12:24   Amplified Bible (AMP)

and to Jesus, the Mediator of a new covenant [uniting God and man], and to the sprinkled blood, which speaks [of mercy], a better *and* nobler *and* more gracious message than *the blood* of Abel [which cried out for vengeance].

1 Peter 1:3   Amplified Bible (AMP)
Blessed [gratefully praised and adored] be the God and
Father of our Lord Jesus Christ, who according to His
abundant *and* boundless mercy has caused us to be born
again [that is, to be reborn from above—spiritually
transformed, renewed, and set apart for His purpose] to
an ever-living hope *and* confident assurance through the
resurrection of Jesus Christ from the dead,

2 John 3   King James Version (KJV)
Grace be with you, mercy, and peace, from God the
Father, and from the Lord Jesus Christ, the Son of the
Father, in truth and love.

Jude 2   Amplified Bible (AMP)
May mercy and peace and love be multiplied to you
[filling your heart with the spiritual well-being and seren-
ity experienced by those who walk closely with God].